WHEN

FAITH

MEETS

THERAPY

WHEN

FAITH

MEETS

THERAPY

FIND HOPE AND A PRACTICAL PATH TO EMOTIONAL, SPIRITUAL, AND RELATIONAL HEALING

ANTHONY EVANS AND STACY KAISER, MA LMFT

WITH JAMIE BLAINE

W PUBLISHING GROUP

AN IMPRINT OF THOMAS NELSON

When Faith Meets Therapy

© 2022 Anthony Evans and Stacy Kaiser

Published in Nashville, Tennessee, by W Publishing, an imprint of Thomas Nelson.

Thomas Nelson titles may be purchased in bulk for educational, business, fund-raising, or sales promotional use. For information, please email SpecialMarkets@ThomasNelson.com.

Unless otherwise noted, Scripture quotations are taken from the Holy Bible, New International Version®, NIV®. Copyright © 1973, 1978, 1984, 2011 by Biblica, Inc.® Used by permission of Zondervan. All rights reserved worldwide. www.Zondervan.com. The "NIV" and "New International Version" are trademarks registered in the United States Patent and Trademark Office by Biblica, Inc.®

Scripture quotations marked AMP are taken from the Amplified® Bible (AMP). Copyright © 2015 by The Lockman Foundation. Used by permission. www.lockman.org

Scripture quotations marked CSB are taken from the Christian Standard Bible®. Copyright © 2017 by Holman Bible Publishers. Used by permission. Christian Standard Bible® and CSB® are federally registered trademarks of Holman Bible Publishers.

Scripture quotations marked ESV are taken from the ESV® Bible (The Holy Bible, English Standard Version®). Copyright © 2001 by Crossway, a publishing ministry of Good News Publishers. Used by permission. All rights reserved.

Scripture quotations marked GNT are taken from the Good News Translation in Today's English Version—Second Edition. Copyright © 1992 by American Bible Society. Used by permission.

Scripture quotations marked KJV are taken from the King James Version. Public domain.

Scripture quotations marked MSG are taken from THE MESSAGE. Copyright © 1993, 2002, 2018 by Eugene H. Peterson. Used by permission of NavPress. All rights reserved. Represented by Tyndale House Publishers, a Division of Tyndale House Ministries.

Scripture quotations marked NASB are taken from the New American Standard Bible® (NASB). Copyright © 1960, 1971, 1977, 1995, 2020 by The Lockman Foundation. All rights reserved. Used by permission. www.Lockman.org

Scripture quotations marked NASB 1995 are taken from the New American Standard Bible® (NASB 1995). Copyright © 1960, 1962, 1963, 1968, 1971, 1973, 1975, 1977, 1995 by the Lockman Foundation. Used by permission. www.Lockman.org

Scripture quotations marked NKJV are taken from the New King James Version®. Copyright © 1982 by Thomas Nelson. Used by permission. All rights reserved.

Scripture quotations marked NLT are taken from the Holy Bible, New Living Translation. Copyright © 1996, 2004, 2015 by Tyndale House Foundation. Used by permission of Tyndale House Ministries, Carol Stream, Illinois 60188. All rights reserved.

Scripture quotations marked NRSV are taken from the New Revised Standard Version Bible. Copyright © 1989 National Council of the Churches of Christ in the United States of America. Used by permission. All rights reserved worldwide.

Some names in the authors' personal stories have been omitted or changed for privacy.

Any internet addresses, phone numbers, or company or product information printed in this book are offered as a resource and are not intended in any way to be or to imply an endorsement by Thomas Nelson, nor does Thomas Nelson vouch for the existence, content, or services of these sites, phone numbers, companies, or products beyond the life of this book.

ISBN 978-0-7852-8977-7 (HC)
ISBN 978-0-7852-8978-4 (TP)
ISBN 978-0-7852-8979-1 (eBook)
ISBN 978-0-7852-8980-7 (audiobook)

Library of Congress Control Number: 2021952958

Printed in the United States of America
22 23 24 25 26 LSC 10 9 8 7 6 5 4 3 2 1

This book is lovingly dedicated to Reyn Danesi, Clint Torres, Tori Kelly, André Murillo, Matt Lashey, Justin Ervin, and Ashley Graham for walking with me so closely and intently when life wasn't easy. Your love, support, and friendship through this recent season is one of the main reasons I've held on to faith and done the emotional work through therapy.

ANTHONY

To my daughters, Jordan and Katie: having you as my children has been the best gift any mother could receive. I love you with all my heart, and I hope that the lessons I have taught you make your journeys as adults a little bit happier and easier.

To Mitch: your love and support go beyond anything that words can express. I am grateful every day to have you in my life.

STACY

"Comfort, oh comfort my people,"
    says your God.
"Speak softly and tenderly to Jerusalem,
    but also make it very clear."

ISAIAH 40:1–2 MSG

CONTENTS

Authors' Note ix

Introduction: The Problem with Algebra xi

1. Jesus and a Therapist 1
2. Add Hope to Your Faith 11
3. Become Your Best Self 23
4. Own It, Then Change It 33
5. Face Your Fear Factor 49
6. Understand the Problems and Purposes of Anger 63
7. Find Grace for Guilt and Shame 77
8. Feel Your Pain to Heal It 89
9. Recognize Your Toxic People 103
10. Release Your Toxic People and Refocus Your Life 119
11. Experience Forgiveness by Letting Go 137
12. Protect Your Peace, Then Live in It 147
13. The Seven Keys to Healthy Relationships 161
14. Grow Through Grief and Loss 175
15. Unleash Your Inner Power 189
16. Change Everything with Gratitude 207

Conclusion: Whatever Comes Your Way 217

Acknowledgments 221

Spiritual Health Resources 223

Mental Health Resources 231

Notes 233

About the Authors 235

AUTHORS' NOTE

When Faith Meets Therapy is not intended to be a substitute for professional advice, diagnosis, or treatment. Always seek the guidance of your mental health professional or other qualified health provider with any questions you may have regarding your condition.

If you are in crisis or think you may have an emergency, call your doctor or 911 immediately. If you are having suicidal thoughts, call 1-800-273-TALK (8255) to talk to a skilled, trained counselor at a crisis center in your area at any time. If you are located outside the United States, call your local emergency line immediately.

THE PROBLEM WITH ALGEBRA

*Where there is no [wise, intelligent] guidance, the people
fall [and go off course like a ship without a helm], but
in the abundance of [wise and godly] counselors there is
victory.*

PROVERBS 11:14 AMP

Anthony

I don't want to assume that everyone who picks up this book knows me, and since this is the introduction to this book, I guess I should introduce myself.

I'm the oldest son of Drs. Lois and Tony Evans from Dallas, Texas. I'm a worship leader, songwriter, and producer living in Dallas and Los Angeles. My mom and dad are the founders of Oak Cliff Bible Fellowship, where my dad, to this day, is still the pastor. They also founded a global ministry called The Urban Alternative, and my dad is the president. I don't know how he had time to do it, but somewhere along the way he has squeezed in writing more than 120 books, including his popular Kingdom series. You may have seen me on the road with my big sister, Priscilla Shirer, a speaker, Bible teacher, author, and occasional actress. I'm also the proud brother of two more amazing and accomplished siblings—authors and speakers Chrystal Evans Hurst and Jonathan Evans.

Although I love the Cali sunshine, I split time between Texas and LA. You see, my mom passed away two years ago, and Priscilla had a serious health scare. The Evans family suffered a lot of tragedy and loss in a very short period of time. Then the pandemic hit. My family needed me, so without hesitation I made sure to be closer to home. Work can wait! Family comes first—*always.*

I enjoy making records, producing vocals, spearheading new ideas for the family, working on television shows, films, and events, and I even get to do some acting now and then. About a decade ago, I was a contestant on *The Voice.* More recently, I played opposite Zooey Deschanel in *Beauty and the Beast in Concert* at the Hollywood Bowl. (Zooey was the beauty.) I'm literally all over the place doing all sorts of things, which suits my— *hey look, squirrel!*—attention span.

I suppose we can add *author* to that list because this is actually my third book after *Unexpected Places* and one with my family titled *Divine Disruption.* But the tone of this one is a little different.

So, why am I writing about mental health? Let me take you back in time a few years.

When I was in ninth grade at Duncanville High School, I remember sitting in math class and being totally lost. Like blindfolded-and-upside-down-underwater clueless. That's the year that math got crazy and turned into algebra.

All these years later, I can still see it and feel it in my chest. Our teacher, Ms. Fratelli, was working out a problem on the board. She had long dark hair and appeared to be just a few years older than us and, looking back now, had some pretty dope style for a schoolteacher. Her gentle voice was so soothing, but occasionally she would stutter while trying to cram in all the principles of algebra before the bell rang and we all scattered.

The equation Ms. Fratelli was working on that morning had so many steps that she had to stand on her toes to fit all those x's and y's and weird symbols on the board. Like n^2 to the power of nine billion squared backward or something like that. It looked like secret alien code downloaded from a faraway galaxy, but when Ms. Fratelli finished it off with an equal sign and a final number, the other kids in class nodded like they understood.

I had no clue how she came up with the final solution. I didn't even understand how she got to the equal sign. Truth is, I got lost all the way back on step two. Nothing on Ms. Fratelli's board made sense to me.

Math is about fundamental truths; I get that. But even though I'd studied the textbook, it felt like I was in so far over my head that I would never be able to understand it or get it to work for me. A problem that takes forty-seven perfectly executed steps to get right? Are you kidding? I'm going to make a mistake somewhere along the way. But I had to pass the class to get out of ninth grade and keep going. I was trapped.

My brain started spinning as anxiety crawled from my heart to my throat, choking off my breath, making me dizzy, like the walls and ceiling were closing in. I wanted to throw that textbook across the room and run out screaming. But I didn't, of course. I just sat there, quiet, squinting at the board and praying for revelation to come.

I had tried to pay closer attention, asking questions when I didn't understand. My hand stayed up so much that Ms. Fratelli finally told me I was holding back the rest of the class. Sometimes, when I asked a question, the other kids would stare at me like I was a milk cow stranded in downtown Dallas traffic. This only made my anxiety worse. Algebra felt like some cruel trick from the pit of hell.

I wanted to quit so badly. But I couldn't. If I was going to survive algebra, I would need special help. I would have to get a tutor.

That's how I look at faith and therapy. For some of us, life is kind of like algebra. We know what the Bible says the solution is supposed to be, but somewhere in the steps to work out the problem, we get overwhelmed and lost. Some of us can't even figure out where to start. I need special help—someone to work with me to break down the problem step by step and help me get unstuck, to move from where I am to where I want and need to be.

There are many times when God's Word makes it clear what we should and should not be doing. He works out the problem for us, and it's more like simple addition and subtraction. I'm not tempted to rob banks or sell drugs in the parking lot of Fuel City. I also know that I need to be a good, kind, thoughtful, generous, and praying person.

It's other things that I struggle with—the ever-changing variables that come with relationships and the balance of taking care of yourself without being selfish, setting boundaries and knowing when to hold on and when to let go. Y'all know what I'm talking about. It's the issues of faith that aren't so black-and-white that break me down.

For some reason, admitting that you need extra help in life has been an issue in evangelical church culture for a long time now. Good Christians are supposed to have all the answers, not more questions. After all, we have the textbook for living, the Bible, as if the Word of God is a collection of quick, simple, bullet-point solutions to every one of life's struggles.

I'm not saying the Bible isn't our guide. Just that, if we are honest, life is strange, messy, and hard, and human nature can be so self-destructive. We all need help and guidance to get through. And sometimes, far too often, church can become another place to put on and pretend.

A few years back, I was at a place in life where I was leading worship and church activities every weekend, smiling and shaking hands. People were opening their hearts, telling me their problems, and looking to me for guidance and advice. I was acting like I had it together, like everything was okay. Things were not okay behind the scenes, though.

Do you know how exhausting it is to constantly pretend like you've got it all together? I felt like a fraud, and as time passed, the situation only became worse, and I began a long, downward spiral into functional depression and anxiety.

But you have to keep going. Stuff it all down and get on the plane. Smile, shake hands, sing another song. Get on another plane and go to another church, stand on another platform. Stuff it all down and keep moving.

One morning, a pastor of a church I was attending in Nashville pulled me to the side. "Anthony," he said, looking me straight in the eyes, "at this rate, you will fall apart in a year."

I stumbled for a reply, but the words would not even come out. He was right and I knew it. Part of what makes a person an artist is the ability to feel everything on a different level. Then, are we supposed to cut those feelings off and act like we're doing better than we really are?

I realized that I could pray the prayers and keep the faith, but if I continued to live in denial and run from my feelings, I would eventually fall to pieces, just like that pastor had said. God had a higher call for me. But going to the high places requires hard work. And I knew I would need good, professional help.

The Bible says, "God resists the proud, but gives grace to the humble" (James 4:6 NKJV). I had to get humble enough to admit, "I need help." Just like with algebra, when I got guidance and put in the work, the weight of anxiety began to lift and I started to make progress. James 2:22 says, "You see that faith was working with his works, and as a result of the works, faith was perfected" (NASB 1995). Adding professional therapy (the work) to my faith made the difference.

I'll be forever grateful that God directed me to Stacy Kaiser, a good tutor and guide. Our working it out together is what we are now so eager to share with you.

This is not a collection of self-help sermons from the pulpit to those gathered in their Sunday best. This book is more Thursday night in your pajamas than Sunday morning suits and fancy dresses. It's a safe place to be who you really are and ask questions, with only acceptance and no judgment.

It's also a book where we will be offering what we call a practical path to emotional, spiritual, and relational healing. This is by way of an honest conversation between a faith leader and a licensed therapist that includes tools, tips, and keys for dealing with life's difficulties. In fact, at the end of most every chapter you'll find "Stacy's Tips to Help You Get Started"—therapeutic tools that prompt reflection, realization, and action to help you on your journey to greater mental and emotional health.

There are plenty of faith-based books out there about how to change your life from sad to happy, be an overcomer, fix your broken relationships, find your calling and purpose, and not be so messed up, depressed, and confused. In our book we want to have an open, honest conversation about faith and mental health in a way that doesn't make a person feel worse about themselves and their relationship with God. Jesus said His burden is light (Matthew 11:30). We were never meant to carry all that weight.

Some may say, "All you need is prayer," but James 2:17 tells us that faith is worthless without works—and work requires tools. Good therapy gives us tools for living a God-honoring and emotionally peaceful life. Good tools are simply biblical principles put into action. All truth is God's truth as we work together for the good.

Life got a lot harder for all of us in the last couple of years. Even the toughest are struggling and fighting to hold on. We need more help, more kindness, more honesty about our private struggles. There's no shame in seeking help, especially if you are going through a war.

The right guidance can help us see our own faults and wrong beliefs and move toward a better, healthier walk with God and others.

Our hope is that my stories and experiences, along with Stacy's expertise, will help you break loose and move forward—or simply find the courage to ask for help.

JESUS SAID HIS BURDEN IS LIGHT. WE WERE NEVER MEANT TO CARRY ALL THAT WEIGHT.

ONE

JESUS AND A THERAPIST

*The purposes of a person's heart are deep waters, but
one who has insight draws them out.*

PROVERBS 20:5

Anthony

One afternoon, I was sitting in my apartment with the sliding glass door
open, letting the breeze blow in. The *Steve Harvey* talk show was on TV,
but I wasn't really paying close attention until an audience member asked
a question about a situation in their life that had become out of control.
Steve had a professional therapist on that afternoon to help with guidance. The therapist listened carefully and calmly offered wisdom into the
situation. Her words were profound but straightforward, cutting through
the drama to the heart of the matter.

I liked that. I *needed* that. I didn't want somebody to tell me what I
wanted to hear because I came from a family of famous preachers. The
therapist seemed down-to-earth, not like someone I'd have to pretend
with. I was tired of pretending.

Her words were so powerful that I watched until the show was over, and when the credits rolled, I got very close to the TV until they showed her name. Then, I went straight to my laptop and googled "Stacy Kaiser." Turns out, she was in Los Angeles, like me.

Stacy's office had a website, and I was so desperate for someone to talk to that I sent an email right then, trying to convince her staff that I wasn't a stalker or some lunatic and could they *please* get me in for an appointment somehow?

Soon?

Stacy

And that's where I came into Anthony's life and, ultimately, into yours. As a child I always had a desire to work in the helping profession. In high school I started referring to this desire as a calling. Since that time, I have used my education, career, and training to work as a therapist with individuals, groups, and corporations; as a college professor; and in the media. As a result, my private practice is rather small and often booked out for weeks or even months at a time.

It was a miracle that I had an opening for an appointment—these days Anthony and I call it a divine intervention. We have a screening process for all first-time appointments, so after my staff spoke with Anthony, we jumped on a call to make sure the conversational chemistry between us was right. From there, we were able to set a time for a face-to-face session the following week.

Anthony

The next Tuesday afternoon, I walked into Stacy's office, super-scared and anxious about opening up, afraid of being judged and of what I might find if I started looking too closely at myself. All that vanished quickly though. Stacy put me at ease. Talking to her was not as difficult as I had imagined. It also helped that she didn't have a clue who I was, what I did, or anything about my family.

Her office was a safe place. I had a clean slate. And as it turned out, our backgrounds were more similar than I might have guessed.

Stacy

When I was in high school, I was a children's Sunday school teacher. It began when I was eleven years old. I was offered a job on Sunday mornings doing everything from taking the little kids to the bathroom to handing out candy. I made one dollar an hour and worked my way up from there to teaching the class.

Teaching Sunday school was likely the foundation for my desire to help others. That, and the fact that my mother worked in a helping profession. I knew that serving others and helping them find their way was a meaningful way to spend a life.

My journey has a lot to do with people working on change within themselves, but faith is an important part of my own life and not disconnected from the work I do. I believe that positive change can come from a relationship with God, the people around us, and from within. My work is focused on empowering people to create change so they can heal and live the kind of life they both deserve and desire.

Anthony

It gave me a huge feeling of relief to know that Stacy understood my background and the importance of faith. Still, therapy was a new experience for me. Honestly, it felt strange to look for help outside of a church setting.

I'm going to share a lot of stories and illustrations in this book because it's the best way I know to explain something. Jesus often told stories to explain things, too, so I guess we're okay. Let me tell you a little bit about how I see Stacy's role in my life.

The other day I went to play tennis with Steven, a good friend of mine. Steven is a naturally gifted athlete, someone who can pick up any sport and before long he's killing it, playing like a pro. Steven was new to tennis, so he hired a coach. As we knocked the ball back and forth, the coach was giving us both tips.

I was trying to hit the ball inside the lines, but my shots were going all over the place—into the net, over the fence. I was putting in a lot of effort but wasn't really making any progress.

"Swing from your hips, Anthony," the coach suggested. "Loosen up, stand easy."

As we played, the coach kept guiding me. "Bend your knees. Follow through on the swing. Like that, yeah. Much better."

Just with those small adjustments, my game improved immediately. I had more power in my swing, more impact and accuracy with the ball. And when I followed the coach's advice, I was less tired because my energy wasn't wasted on bad form or technique.

That's what working with Stacy was like. I had a coach on the sidelines of my life, watching and giving me tips that were in line with my goals. Giving small corrections and adjustments so I could live more intentionally as an emotionally healthy believer and not waste a lot of time and energy while half my shots went over the fence or into the ground.

Before I met with Stacy, I had lost the confidence that I could be any good in certain areas of my life. She helped me clean up my swing and build up the self-assurance and belief that I could move forward. The truth is, *I can* be in healthy relationships. *I can* manage my anxiety. *I can* rid myself of codependent tendencies and be strategically intentional in my ministry and career. I can do this crazy life thing and be okay.

Stacy

Like I said earlier, faith has always been a strong part of my personal and professional life. But I find it interesting that while I was helping

Anthony improve his life, he helped enhance mine by encouraging me to work with him on the *When Faith Meets Therapy* project.

Before we dive in, I think it is important to offer this additional disclaimer: *working with a therapist is a confidential relationship.* Anthony is making it known that we work together, but the specific details that you will hear about his personal life are coming from him. He has asked for me to be a part of this process and to provide my insight, but know that I will not be breaking any client confidentiality—we will only be sharing *our own* experiences and stories. The discussion points here have all been approved by him.

Early in our sessions, Anthony began to tell me about his family and background with faith. In my mind, the combination of faith and therapy has always been a perfect match, and so it was easy for me to talk with him about what he might expect from therapy. In our work together we would focus on dealing with emotional wellness, but he still needed to make sure that he was using his faith to hold on to his spiritual well-being.

It is important to understand that therapy is not a replacement for your spiritual work or connection. It's an enhancement for that, and no counselor should ever criticize or downplay the role of faith in your life. I have had a few people in my life question the therapy process. They saw this type of counseling as some sort of mysterious voodoo practice, like we therapists are first cousins to palm readers and psychics.

Sure, there are bad therapists out there, but in the way that there are poor practitioners in every profession—bad therapists, hairdressers, lawyers, pastors, teachers, and . . . you get it! A good therapist, regardless of what they believe personally, should encourage you in your faith and be completely supportive and even encouraging of your seeking additional help and guidance from spiritual leaders and those connected to your faith.

Anthony and I talk a lot about God and faith in our sessions because that's a huge part of his life. A good therapist gives you lots of space to talk about all facets of your life, from family, to work, to faith and more. With reference to his tennis analogy, I try to help him take an objective look at his life and relationships while adjusting his swing so he can have a better connection with himself, his friends, his family, and God.

Anthony

It's amazing to have a great coach guiding me from the sidelines of life. This just makes me want to play that much harder.

Is it too soon to tell another story? I think most of us love stories, and again, I have plenty of them.

As a professional singer, I have been blessed to sing on stages around the world. Most singers used to use a wedge monitor, which is a speaker box that sits at the front of the stage to reflect your voice back to you. It's difficult to stay on time and in tune if you cannot hear yourself.

But every venue is different. Sometimes the drums are too loud or there's an echo or too much keyboard in the mix. The show must go on, so as a singer in the midst of a performance, you have to do your best and strain to hear yourself over the noise.

Have you ever seen a singer turn away from the crowd and stick their finger in their ear? That means they can't hear themselves.

That used to happen to me all the time, and I was blowing out my voice and straining my vocal cords. It came to the point where I required surgery and was placed on complete vocal rest for months.

Finally, I got the monitors that go inside my ears. That way I don't have to strain to hear my voice above the noise. Stacy was like my in-ear monitor. She provided instruction and helped me do the work that in turn provided a clearer way of hearing myself over the noise, without the echo or other competing voices drowning me out. I get a more pure and accurate reflection of what is going on around me so I can stay "in tune" and connected with myself and the Lord. Being situated in a place where the volume of your emotions is under control allows you to hear God's heart for you more clearly. And when you start to hear His heart, you will simultaneously begin to hear the truth about who you are.

It's so much easier to hear God's voice, to stay in tune and experience internal harmony, when we cut through the noise of life. Everyone requires help with that at some point or another. We all need good monitors. Jesus talked about seeing the speck in someone else's eye while we're nearly going blind from all the junk in our own (Matthew 7:5). It's so much easier to point out other people's problems than focus on finding and fixing our own.

Our hope is that this book will help you cut through and quiet life's noise so you can hear your own voice and, more importantly, God's.

Stacy

One of the things Anthony and I both know is that there have been plenty of times when faith has been enough to get us through. But there are other situations where you need some extra assistance. If you struggle with math, it's smart to get an accountant to take care of your taxes. There's no shame in seeking assistance, whether it is with financial, physical, spiritual, or emotional needs. And after all, no one person knows everything about everything, so why not turn to someone who is an expert in the field to guide you down a difficult path?

Anthony

In the same way, if you struggle with a physical ailment, you need to pray and seek both God and a good physician to get your situation under control. So why not Jesus and a therapist?

Something I eventually realized, with Stacy's help, is that God gave me an artist's heart. I can write songs and sing them and make people feel something inside. But the price of having that ability is that it also means that I am easily overwhelmed by emotions.

Not that I would want to be bold enough to compare myself to David in the Bible, but for real, every time I read the Psalms I empathize with and feel him so much. He was constantly torn between his emotions and the truth, his circumstances and the reality of the God he served. That is me *all* the time! I truly believe that artists rarely experience creativity without the turmoil of trying to keep their beautiful and chaotic emotions under control.

Sometimes, in faith communities, sensitivity and emotion are mistaken for weakness. For years I tried to hide, deny, or change the fact that I was an emotional person because it was so uncomfortable to me. But you know what? I could not hide, deny, or change who I was. That was like a horse trying not to run or a lion trying not to roar. Emotion was natural to me, and it only made things harder and worse when I tried to deny the essence of who I was.

What I *could* do is try to understand my emotions and not let them run wild and wreck my life. That was a much better solution. Knowing the solution didn't make getting there any easier, though. It took a lot of help, guidance, work, and taking a long, hard look at my thoughts and behaviors.

But now that I am healthier, I am better able to help others too. Leading worship and making music brings me joy, but I believe that I am just as called to help those who are struggling with emotional pain, loss, depression, or anxiety.

Stacy

A lot of people have asked me if therapists tell you how to live your life. They aren't supposed to do that, since only you truly know what is best for you and your situation. Instead, we are trained to be objective listeners with special tools who help guide you into figuring out the best way to heal your pain and navigate challenges so you can achieve the life you are trying to build.

And we don't need to have walked in your shoes to offer guidance and support; instead, we are trained to get a sense of the shoes you are walking in and help you through that understanding. One of the great things about a good therapist is that we are not running an agenda. Often, even the most well-meaning friend or family member is guiding you in a direction that they think is best—not one that is necessarily best for you.

Even I have had to deal with the occasional friend or family member who is trying to push me into doing or saying something that isn't right for me. These well-meaning people don't realize that they are not helpful and that sometimes their behavior makes us stop reaching out for support. Plus, many of us tend to isolate during tough times, afraid to ask for help because we don't want to share or we fear being a burden. One of my goals in writing this book is to help you overcome all that—to know that it is healthy and important to reach out for help.

Anthony

We all are so different. For instance, my dad, Dr. Tony Evans, can quote any Bible verse about any subject, Old Testament or New. But he is simply not a highly emotional person. God did not make him that way. So, even though I am Anthony Evans Jr. and I have my father's name, I did not inherit his emotional makeup. My struggles are not his, and vice versa.

I fought against that idea for a long time, trying to stuff down how I felt, trying to deny the way things would impact me, trying to pray or move past it all. Eventually, Stacy helped me understand that I couldn't ignore emotions. To get to the other side of them, I had to work through them and come to terms with the fact that God intentionally made me this way.

But she also taught me that you can trust the work. The way out is not around the valley. It's through it.

THERAPY IS NOT A REPLACEMENT FOR YOUR SPIRITUAL WORK OR CONNECTION. IT'S AN ENHANCEMENT.

◻ TWO ◻

ADD HOPE TO YOUR FAITH

Faith is the substance of things hoped for, the evidence of things not seen.

HEBREWS 11:1 KJV

Anthony

There was a point a few years ago when it seemed like I was living the dream. I had a place in Los Angeles and was busy with big projects and important ministry events, standing on stages and singing hope-filled songs. At the time I couldn't explain why I felt so sad, but I did. I was only going through the motions. On the outside I sang with confidence, but on the inside I had lost hope.

I know what it feels like to not be able to get out of bed in the morning. I've had days and weeks when I could not pray or work or praise the dark clouds away. I know what it's like to be exhausted and depressed all the time, for sleep to not be restful and food to have no taste. I know what it's like to feel hope slipping away until it seems you've hit rock bottom—then the next day a whole new rock bottom awaits.

That's hard for me to say. But if you want to help people, and I do, you have to be willing to be open, honest, and real. You need to be transparent. You cannot hide your scars and reach the hurting at the same time. You must be willing to talk about the pain.

Stacy

To me, faith is believing something without full proof, and hope is your attitude toward that belief. Faith and hope are two things we can hold on to when we are struggling to make it through the hardest parts in life. Especially in times of tragedy and loss.

Faith and hope in God and yourself are the foundations on which we build a healthy life. When those parts of us are shaky, as they were for Anthony at that hard time, we need to spend time and effort to stabilize them.

Having faith and hope is also important when selecting a therapist. You must have hope in those you look to for guidance and faith that they will be able to help you. Hope and faith also require trust. Trust takes time. Anthony and I had a good connection to start with, but it took a lot of sessions before we were able to go to the truly deep places and openly talk about his underlying issues and pain.

Anthony

I had tried talking with someone before. At one point, I reached out to a church-based counselor for help. I was so excited and ready to work on myself that I went in there with blind faith and poured my heart out for an hour straight.

At the end of the session, the counselor stood, shook my hand, and said, "Man, I love the work of your family, especially your father. Could you get me connected to him? I would really like to join my ministry with his."

I was so shocked that I couldn't even find the words to reply. I actually remember balling up my fists in anger. *Like, really? For real? You're supposedly a professional counselor with degrees on the wall and the only thing you can think about is using my pain and desperation to further your career?* I left his office more disillusioned and depressed than before.

If you need open-heart surgery and find a Spirit-filled doctor who prays, then hallelujah. But make sure he's a quality surgeon as well. Unfortunately, the label "Christian" is far too often an excuse to offer second-rate work from someone with little to no training. There are a lot of professional, competent counselors out there who also follow the Lord. So choose quality *and* capability, not just a service that's advertised as Christian.

At times I struggle with anxiety, but I don't need to pay a church counselor seventy-five dollars an hour to remind me that the Bible says, "Be anxious for nothing" (Philippians 4:6 NKJV). You don't think I have quoted that verse ten thousand times, morning, noon, and night, before I came for help? The problem is, I know the verse and still struggle with anxiety—so what's wrong with me? Is God mad? Am I crazy? Why can't I make the truth of God's Word work in my life?

My experience with that therapist reminded me of the Bible story where Jesus was hungry and saw a fig tree in the distance. But when He got closer, the tree was barren (Mark 11:13). I came tired and hopeful, but the tree didn't offer any fruit. I walked away just as hungry as before.

After that session, I sort of gave up. I figured any therapist or spiritual leader I might go to looking for help would know my family. There would be too much pressure to perform or use my connections to help build their brand.

But pain has a way of changing your mind. I couldn't give up.

Stacy

Anthony's experience with the church-based counselor was a disappointing one. As I mentioned earlier, just as there are good and bad doctors, there are good and bad therapists. Some faith-based counselors are excellent, but there are others who do more harm than good.

Anthony sets a good example. If you don't get what you want or need, or if you feel uncomfortable, keep looking. It's essential to find a professional who not only has the training but also communicates and connects with you in a way that is helpful.

Anthony

Thank God I found the right therapist because a few years later, my life really got crazy. We lost eight family members in a very short time, including my grandfather and mom. I moved back to Dallas and watched my mother's health fade away even in an incredible atmosphere of hope and faith-filled prayers.

These were precious times, and I wouldn't have wanted to be anywhere else when Mommy passed—but it was the hardest thing I have ever had to do. Then, Priscilla, my sister, had her own battle with a cancerous tumor in her lungs. Shortly after, COVID hit. Things were stressful, to say the least.

Stacy

The pandemic has left most of us with some symptoms of post-traumatic stress disorder. Isolation, fear, sickness, financial problems, the loss of friends and family members. Anthony experienced a pileup of both pain and trauma. In challenging situations like these, faith and hope give us strength to persevere.

Anthony

At times, in traumatic situations, you have to make a decision to let some things go. You simply cannot carry everything at one time. In my case, the first thing to go was my physical health. The Deep South is a lot different from West Los Angeles. They don't mind if you look a little "thick," so the next thing you know I was relaxing and enjoying myself a bit too much and could no longer fit in my clothes.

Once the lockdowns loosened up, I found a good nutritionist to help get me back on track. I knew all the principles of healthy eating. Grilled salmon, leafy greens—I get all that. But having the knowledge was not enough. I needed someone to walk beside me and share their insight and knowledge. So on those days in Texas when I'm tempted to give in and pig out on biscuits and gravy and chicken-fried steak, I can lean on the words and the experience of my nutritionist. That gives me the strength to make better choices.

I got to a place where I was tracking everything that I was eating so I could focus on reaching my goals. This is a bit like how Stacy constantly tells me to "check in with myself." It's her way of reminding me to keep an account of my emotions and what message they are sending me.

There will be times when we need an independent source to remind us that the quality of our lives largely depends on the quality of our choices. Experience has taught me that I can have faith in good choices. And with that faith comes hope.

Still, there's a balance. You can't be too hard on yourself either.

Stacy

Often I will reach out through my social media and let people know that I am taking questions. I get a lot of replies asking how to stay hopeful in difficult circumstances.

When life is unfair or you're worn out or the bad news just keeps coming, it is normal to feel like your hope has gone out the window—with your faith right behind it. And even though you might know that hope is important to faith and emotional well-being, sometimes you just cannot figure out how to get there.

In these tough times, maybe you are angry, hurting, or sad. That's where someone like me comes in. You can know the right thing to do, and yet the feelings of hopelessness can cause you to struggle to get it done. Ultimately, we all want to be our best selves. God is in line with those desires, but sometimes it takes an outside perspective to accomplish that goal.

Anthony

I am reminded of Hebrews 11:1, which says, "Faith is the substance of things hoped for, the evidence of things not seen" (KJV).

When you begin to hope, and in turn add quality decisions to that hope, your faith will become tangible. It's seeing and believing in your heart before you see and believe in your physical reality. It's what we do when we decide we like someone. We hope that they might feel the same way, so we start taking steps toward the reality we want. The difference between a romantic relationship and one with God is that He promises when we move toward Him, He will undoubtedly do the same (James 4:8).

Stacy

Hope is alive and thriving inside of us from the moment we are born.

As infants, we cry out to our caregivers in the hope that we will be comforted with a bottle or a breast and the gentle, soothing motion of rocking back and forth. As young children, most of us wake every day hopeful that we will get to go to a friend's house after school or have that special treat after dinner. Holidays are particularly special to children as we live with the hopes of wished-for toys or birthday parties, tooth fairies, trick-or-treat, an Easter basket filled with chocolate candies.

In adolescence we hope our crushes will notice us, for a driver's license and car, that the right college will let us in. As young adults we go to grand efforts in hopes of finding our life partners, being financially stable, and building a solid family structure. And in midlife we hope for things like career advancement, to buy our dream homes, that our families will be healthy and secure.

Hope evolves and changes throughout our lives, but the feeling remains the same. We hope because that's what humans do. It is the fuel that keeps us energized and moving forward.

In my many years of experience, I have discovered that people who live in a state of hopefulness tend to be more motivated and adventurous, with a stronger sense of self-worth and contentment. Hopeful people have more satisfaction in their careers and relationships. They live longer and have more friends.

But we live in a challenging world, and hope can take a beating. Some turn up their noses at the very concept of hope. To them, *hopeful* refers to some naive, wide-eyed, overly blissful person who has no clue about the realities of life.

This isn't true. The hopeful are not oblivious. They are passionate, optimistic, and dedicated to their beliefs and their ability to bring about positive change. While a "hopeful" outlook can be a hardwired character trait, the hard knocks of life can cause even the most positive-thinking person to lose hope.

But I believe that no matter who you are, hope is a fire that never goes out. While it may grow dim and cold, the embers remain. If you are feeling hopeless, that can change. *You* can change. You just need to figure out how to reignite the flames.

Hope is related to your perceptions about yourself, others, and the world around you. Deep down, if you still believe that good things can happen, that life still has possibilities, and that you can find a way to make positive changes, you've got a place to begin.

It begins with small changes. Setting goals that are realistic and within reach, keeping a mindset that is open to new options, identifying and rallying support. Maybe your goal was to read one chapter of this book today. Maybe it was simply to get out of bed and wash your hair. Start small. Start where you are. The human brain strives for success. Success breeds success. Small steps create motivation for larger ones.

Anthony asked for a few steps to start cultivating hope in his life, and this is how I answered. They are three steps you can take too.

1. **TAKE A MOMENT TO THINK ABOUT YOUR HOPES AND DREAMS.** What's missing in your life? How are you unfulfilled? Want a promotion at work? A mate? To get more physically, emotionally, or spiritually healthy? Maybe purchase a home? Make a hope list, then break down each item on your list into smaller pieces. Ask yourself, *What can I do today that will get me closer to this goal?* Maybe it looks something like this:

   Goal: Build my financial stability.
   - Read up on or consult an expert on how to build financial stability.
   - Make a budget to include a plan of spending, saving, and giving.
   - Think about traumas or emotional baggage that have impacted spending and saving habits, then work on healing those.

   See? It doesn't have to be giant steps. Your day will end better knowing that you even made half an inch of progress toward your goals. That's how hope is born. Tiny victories, bundled together until hope and confidence grows. Enough tiny victories can outweigh the occasional defeat.

2. **JOIN A GROUP.** Volunteer. Find ways to be in an environment of optimism with people who will build you up. Yes, sometimes we have to fake it until we make it. Some groups are awkward, and sometimes we are drawn to enthusiastic, outgoing people only to discover they're trying to rope us into a pyramid scheme. Refuse to let it derail your efforts. Losing hope is a bigger disability than losing one's leg.

3. **MAKE A HOPE JAR.** Fill your jar with slips of paper of things you want to do. Small things are fine. Learn to bake like the chefs on the Food Network. Organize your home. Rescue a pet. And if you want to make a hope slip that says, "Take a nap," that's okay too. Too much ambition can be just as stress inducing as too much lethargy.

As a therapist, I am often asked how I endure so many stories of heartache, loss, and pain. It is because in every situation, I see hope. I have witnessed lives change. I have watched as people heal, hearts mend, laughter returns, and hope is born again. And I am energized by those moments.

Anthony

More than likely we've all heard the saying, "Without hope the people perish." That quote is inspired by Proverbs 29:18, "Where there is no vision, the people perish" (KJV). Vision gives you hope of a destination. When you see the map on your phone, it gives you an actual picture of your destination although you aren't there yet. You start moving toward it with the hope of eventually arriving because you saw it first.

This is also true with faith. Hope that shows itself as faith truly sets our hearts, minds, and in turn, our emotions toward healing.

It's so clear that we need both faith and hope. But we also need help to know how to integrate these important things into our lives so we can become whole emotionally, spiritually, and relationally.

As I mentioned in the introduction to this book, at the end of the chapters, Stacy has included tips to help you find a pathway through your own life challenges. Many of these are the same thoughts and questions I worked through. They led me toward being free to experience the depth of peace the Lord had for me.

—————— STACY'S TIPS TO HELP YOU GET STARTED

- **REFLECTION:** The reflection phase of healing is about looking back on who you are and the coping skills you have picked up throughout your life. In terms of *hope*, think about when and why you began to lose hope. Was it in response to circumstances within your control or outside of it? Ask yourself what you have learned in your past about how to handle things when life feels hopeless. Take steps to consider and start to understand where each of these events landed and the lasting impact they've had in your life.

- **REALIZATION:** Take note of the realizations that you had while reflecting. Put them into a journal, computer, or smartphone, and consider sharing them with a counselor. Understanding the source of any hopelessness is important. If you are feeling hopeless because of something that was out of your control, give yourself grace and remind yourself that sometimes life is hard, and we can only take control of things that we can actually control.

- **ACTION:** In the action phase of healing, it is time to take steps to change what you can control. Interestingly enough, as we begin to become aware of what we *can* change, we begin to feel more hope, and so any feelings of hopelessness should start to fade once these steps are taken.

  - Make a promise to yourself that you will control what you can control and leave the uncontrollable things to God.
  - It is important to write down some small and large steps that you can start to take to build your sense of hopefulness. If you have felt hopeless about finances, relationships, your job, or any part of life, begin to write down steps you can take to help improve those areas of your life.
  - Then share those steps with a trusted family member, friend, or counselor so your plans can be witnessed and supported.

HOPE IS A FIRE THAT NEVER GOES OUT.

THREE

BECOME YOUR BEST SELF

Don't copy the behavior and customs of this world, but let God transform you into a new person by changing the way you think. Then you will learn to know God's will for you, which is good and pleasing and perfect.

ROMANS 12:2 NLT

Anthony

Recently I was watching the Olympics—the 2020 Olympics that we had to hold in 2021. Gymnastics is just crazy to me. Those athletes are superhuman. I can't even wrap my head around the things they can make their bodies do.

During these last Olympic Games, everybody's eyes were on American gymnast Simone Biles. The announcers talked as if every other competitor was an Olympic hopeful, but Simone, she was a sure thing. There was no doubt that when the games were over, she would be on that platform, more than likely listening to "The Star-Spangled Banner" while biting on gold.

23

During the team gymnastics event, Simone made her approach to the vault, sprang up into the air and . . . awkwardly stopped twisting midair and landed on the mat with an uncharacteristic stumble. Shocked, I took a deep breath and shook my head in disbelief. Simone *always* nails it. It was so out of character for her.

In the slow-motion replay you could see it in her eyes. She was lost in the air, spinning, scared of how she would land. The world would learn that gymnasts call this the "twisties," but I already knew about that—I had seen it before.

My sister Priscilla took gymnastics when we were kids. She was my ride to school, so I would have to go with her to tumbling practice after school. Eventually I became the cameraman so she could study her moves on the playback and improve. Except back then, you didn't just hold up your phone. The Evans family had one of those giant JVC video cameras that weighed about thirty pounds and sat on your shoulder.

Anyway, Priscilla was learning how to do something called a "full," which is a backflip with a full twist. I had this monster camera on my shoulder with the time and date flashing in the viewfinder as Priscilla sprinted down the runway, hit a roundoff into a back handspring, jumped high into the air, and then . . . nothing except for flailing arms. First, she landed on her head, then her feet flew over and bent her neck back before she crumpled in a pile off to the side.

Thankfully, she was practicing in the foam pit, so she didn't break her neck. But it was pretty crazy looking. Priscilla staggered to her feet, looked at the camera, and said, "I got lost." I've got this all on video. Maybe one day I'll upload it to YouTube. (Kidding, 'Silla.)

Priscilla had been in gymnastics for a few years by that time. Even at her level, she knew what she was doing. Simone Biles is a world-record-holding Olympic legend, one of the all-time best. She had hit that vault a thousand times. But despite both of their abilities, something in their minds short-circuited. They still got lost.

I've experienced the twisties too. I have been leading worship and singing since I was in my teens. But I came to a place where I was too much in my head, overthinking things, getting lost and confused, crumpling, flailing, scared of where I might land.

Just because you get lost doesn't mean you aren't capable. And just like Simone Biles, I had to take a step back because it was dangerous for me to continue. Regardless of what people thought, I had to stop before I got hurt. I mean, Jesus Himself had to take time to avoid being overwhelmed and lost in the intensity of His own life and ministry (Mark 1:35; Luke 5:16).

The Bible says to guard your heart and renew your mind daily (Proverbs 4:23; Romans 12:2). That means sometimes, when things begin to break down, you've got to bring your heart and mind to a stop so you can regroup and repair. Some of us have pushed past injury, through the twisties, and found ourselves in a place where serious damage could occur.

Stacy

As usual, Anthony hit the nail on the head with his great description of this debilitating gymnastics phenomenon known as the twisties. Let's talk more about the psychological aspects of what's going on.

The twisties come from feeling anxious, worried, insecure, or uncertain. And our feelings come from the way we think about a particular person, place, or situation. The strange thing is that sometimes we don't even realize that we are thinking something because the thoughts come so fast, or we might be dealing with the results of a traumatic experience.

How we think impacts how we feel and how we behave. If you are thinking, *I am confident, I'm talented, I'm at my best,* then you will feel confident, happy, and joyful, and your behaviors will be positive as well.

On the other hand, if your thoughts are filled with negative messages such as *I can't do this, I've had a bad day, I am such a wreck,* you will feel frustrated, insecure, and sad, and your actions will follow those feelings. As bad as it can feel to receive negativity from someone else, your worst enemy can live right between your own two ears.

I don't know Simone Biles or what was going on in her head, but her thoughts and feelings obviously influenced her actions to the point that she had to step down from the world's most elite and prestigious competition. Based on what I have seen and heard in the media, this was a good decision for her well-being.

Sometimes, all the opportunity and training in the world cannot guarantee our best performance in life. Sometimes we need to step out of the arena, so to speak, and acknowledge what's going on in our hearts and heads. Therapy intervenes on the mental and emotional level so a person can return to a healthy, productive state and become the best version of themself.

Anthony

I understand that in some scenarios it is best for us to take a break. But what can you do when your mind is sabotaging you? When you have taken the break and know the truth but cannot seem to execute it?

Stacy

In cases like that, we need to look at the possibility that we are holding ourselves back.

I believe we all have an innate desire to be our best and feel our best. As young children we learn to roll, crawl, and walk, and then to use those skills to go after things we desire—a toy, a cookie, a caregiver. As we get older, we encounter experiences that either make us try harder or stop trying altogether, which is where self-sabotage comes in.

Self-sabotaging thoughts can come from a few different places: the things that we have learned growing up, our experiences and knowledge as we have grown, and the baggage we have picked up along the way.

To get out of it, we must catch ourselves in the act of self-sabotage.

From there we need to ask ourselves, *What am I thinking and feeling that is contributing to the state that I am in right now?* It's important to identify troubling thoughts before we can work on changing them. (We'll talk more about this in the action portion at the end of this chapter.)

Of course, becoming your best self is not just about avoiding self-sabotage but working to feel strong and confident in as many areas of your life as possible. Work on building your physical, mental, emotional, and spiritual strength so you are ready and able to grow, change, and thrive—no matter what life throws at you.

Anthony

The Bible is clear on what our overall direction should be for living our best lives: to avoid conforming to worldly ideas about who we're supposed to be and to be transformed by truth from the inside out (Romans 12:2). Our growth starts to fall apart, though, when we forget God's Word and what we were ultimately created for.

Our thought lives get the twisties.

That's when we have to figure out ways to begin moving from chaos back into order, from darkness to light. It always requires intentional work on the things we have control over, and it often also requires a guide.

I remember going to a doctor when I was about seven or eight years old. My parents were freaking out. "Anthony can't breathe like he's supposed to," they told the doctor. "Something's wrong. He can't catch his breath."

The doctor ran a series of diagnostic tests and told my folks, "Your son has severe asthma. Breathing is something he's going to have to work on, but with some treatment, he should be just fine."

First, we had to figure out what the problem was. Second, I had to work with professionals to get my asthma under control. It wasn't a quick fix. It took medication and exercises. We figured out the best path for me, but the lesson seemed to be that there were things that were out of my control (asthma), so I had to work on the things that were under my control (meds, building up my lungs) to move forward. Once I got a handle on my condition, I could get back to living a normal life.

Back then, I had no idea that getting my asthma under control was setting me up for a career in music. Can you imagine all the blessing I would have missed if I had left my breathing issues unaddressed?

I see therapy the same way. In a sense, I was struggling to breathe in life. I had to go to a professional to get diagnosed and then follow a plan of treatment so I could breathe and think right again.

Stacy

The good thing about counseling is it's something you only do once or maybe twice a week (if you are in a real crisis), but doing it empowers you to make the most of the rest of your time. Counseling is not magic. I can listen and offer insights and guidance, but really, it comes down to you doing the hard work of change, of working on your own thoughts and beliefs in a way that moves toward a healthier, fuller life.

Anthony

Taking action like that starts in the mind. Our minds impact our performance. Believing and applying spiritual truth affects the mental, which is manifested in the physical. It's like how the Bible says all things work together for the good (Romans 8:28). It's all connected. And just like an athlete who gets their mental condition in line with their physical condition, once we get our spirits in order with our minds and start believing the truth, it will have a ripple effect in every area of our lives—friends, family, work, finances. Everything.

Stacy

When it comes to working on yourself, you are the only person who is with you 24 hours a day, 7 days a week, 365 days a year. We are all alone with our thoughts and must take responsibility of managing our mental health so we can live intentionally.

Anthony

"Do what you can, and God will do what you can't." Joyce Meyer said those words at one of her conferences where I had the privilege of singing. I've never had the opportunity to tell her how that one sentence set in motion my taking responsibility for managing my spiritual and mental health in the ways I could, while having faith that God would do the rest. I want you to understand that truth and take the first step in doing what you can.

—————— STACY'S TIPS TO HELP YOU GET STARTED

- **REFLECTION:** The reflection phase of becoming your best self begins with getting very clear about who you are and who you want to be. Make a list of your strengths and weaknesses so you can begin to know what skills you have and which ones you need to work on. Ask yourself what brings you happiness and what brings you disappointment. It might even be helpful to talk to trusted family or friends and ask them to help you reflect, as they may have thoughts about how you can better your life.
- **REALIZATION:** The reflections from above should help you come to realizations about yourself. For example, I had a client, who I will call Dominique, who reflected on her life and really got in touch with the fact that she hated her job. She also realized what a huge love she had for animals and that she barely spent enough time with her aging parents. These kinds of realizations should always lead to the next step: action.
- **ACTION:** Take these small actions today:

  - Ask yourself what is within your power to make your life better, and then ask yourself what steps you need to take to start that process.

- Make a physical or mental list of the small and large steps you need to take to get there. For example, my client Dominique knew that her job would provide her money to rescue a couple of dogs to express her love of animals. She also decided to start looking into ways to make money while also being around animals, promising herself that once she found something, she would leave the workplace that made her so unhappy. Additionally, she made a plan to visit her family in the coming months so they all would have something to look forward to. Just from those small steps, life improved and she was energized to take more steps.

We don't become our best selves all at once, but by one determined action after another.

JUST BECAUSE YOU GET LOST DOESN'T MEAN YOU AREN'T CAPABLE.

FOUR

OWN IT, THEN CHANGE IT

I've tried everything and nothing helps. I'm at the end
of my rope. Is there no one who can do anything for me?
Isn't that the real question? The answer, thank God, is
that Jesus Christ can and does.

ROMANS 7:24–25 MSG

Anthony

On my days off, there's nothing I love to do more than get a cup of coffee and drive around Dallas or Los Angeles and look at real estate that's for sale. You know those fixer-upper shows on TV? That's my secret dream. I want to be on Magnolia Network with Chip and Joanna Gaines, buying old houses, turning them around and restoring them to things of beauty and function. I don't know—maybe I'll call it *Make It Sing!* or *Singing and Selling.* I guess now that I put it in a book, my dream isn't so secret anymore. (Call me, Chip and Jo!)

Bottom line is, when I see a house I love, I don't focus on the chipped paint, crumbling roof, or waist-high weeds by the front stoop. I see that old run-down house for all the potential it has to become someone's forever home. But regardless of how big my vision might be, I can't just march in there with a sledgehammer and start knocking down walls. Before I can make any changes, I have to own it first.

Becoming the owner of a house is a process. There's a mountain of paperwork and financial approval, Realtors and lawyers and bankers. It's a lot of work. But once you sign those papers and take ownership, you can start remodeling and making a house into what you've dreamed.

That's what I had to do before I could start remodeling my life. I had to own my behaviors, my thoughts, and the responsibility for making change. I could not blame my circumstances or childhood or any of those factors outside of myself. I had to accept myself as God accepted me: just as I am, right where I am. That is where true progress must always begin.

And of course, it takes a lot of courage and grit. Tearing down is a lot easier than building up something that functions, but that's where the beauty lies—in the hope and vision. Change requires investment.

But there is a visceral excitement about change and remodeling when you believe in the vision of what it could become. Like a high-end designer, God has given us a picture in His Word of what a transformed life could look like. The anticipation for that life outweighs any fear or hesitation about the work required to get there. It actually can make the work exciting.

Real estate is a fairly safe investment. Land is a limited and indestructible resource. They're not going to make any more of it, and it's not duplicable. Because of that, the land will likely increase in value.

The Bible tells us that we are a limited resource. Each of us is a one-of-a-kind treasure who is fearfully and wonderfully made and of great value to our Maker (Psalm 139:13–14). Just as God charged Adam with tending to the land in the garden of Eden, when we understand our intrinsic value, we become better stewards of our minds, bodies, and souls.

Stacy

Ownership is easy to understand when we're talking about real estate but not so much when we talk about ourselves. What does it mean? And why is it so important? Simply this: you must take ownership over your life so you can find true happiness and fulfillment. I find it interesting that many of us take better care of the tangible items we own, like cars, homes, and computers, than we take of ourselves.

When it comes to readjusting and taking ownership, I love the concept of remodeling our lives! It is something that can be done on a daily, weekly, monthly, or yearly basis. I am one of those people who checks in on myself regularly. I ask myself how I am feeling, if I am happy, and I assess areas where I would like to grow. I encourage you to try checking in with yourself in this same way so you can monitor how you are doing and adjust things as needed. In my book *How to Be a Grown Up*, I talk in more detail about how to assess your life, but here I'll briefly suggest that you examine all the most important areas of your life, such as family, intimate relationships, career, faith, and finances.

Anthony

I like Stacy's list—those things really are the important areas of our lives. I'd consider those to be the foundation, framework, electrical, and plumbing aspects of a home renovation. There's nothing worse than being in a home that looks cozy and inviting at first glance but has numerous unattended issues beneath the surface.

I had an HGTV-wannabe moment of my own when I bought a house that needed fixing and then attempted to do it myself. Let me just say it's a whole lot easier "watched" than done. As I described earlier, after the transfer of ownership, it was time to get down to what was really going on inside the structure. I had to get behind the veneer—the floors and walls that had been constructed to cover the foundation, framework, electrical, and plumbing aspects of the home, the parts that made it functional. It was a bigger mess than I had anticipated, but that didn't mean I could just cover it back up, slap on a new coat of paint, and call it good. I had some work to do.

I also couldn't blame the previous owner or even the guy who sold the house to me. I not only had to own the property with a legal title, I had to do what I'd come to do. Dig into what was there, work on it, and restore it to the best version of itself. It was a journey, but not unlike the journey we all need to take to see, own, and work on what's behind the veneer of our own lives.

So how do we take these basic principles and apply them to our lives? I know Stacy talks about taking a journey to discover what's on the inside, but how do we actually do that?

Stacy

Yes, it is a journey. I realize that certain phrases like "the journey of self-discovery" might sound odd and suspicious for believers. (Again, part of the purpose of this book is to show that these basic therapeutic principles can help anyone take the appropriate initial steps, regardless of what and how they believe.) Let's not worry about terms but get into the practical process of becoming our best selves.

A prime example of unharnessed, unrealized power is people who do not have a clue who they are. They ramble through life, trying different jobs and mates and places to live, forever changing their external conditions to keep from having to work on themselves because they are afraid of what they might find inside. They're running from their own shadow, you could say.

A person needs to understand their strengths and weaknesses, and that's no easy task. That might require some assistance. We are not here to run an extended commercial for the benefits of therapy, but assistance is part of what quality counseling provides. It holds up a mirror to help you see who you are, what you're doing, how you think and feel, and how those thoughts and feelings influence your actions.

That's why it's so important to surround yourself with people who support your being strong and want to help you succeed at being your very best. Avoid those who criticize you and make you feel weak. And of course strive to avoid being critical and predatory to yourself.

One key in moving toward change is to counteract your weaknesses through utilizing your strengths. Let's say you're having a hard time finding a job but are a highly social person. Use that strength. Talk to everyone you know, meet new people, network, and ask others to help you connect with potential employers.

Recently I had a client who was always getting herself into awkward situations because she couldn't say no to the demands of family, coworkers, and friends. But this person was very detail oriented and kept a daily planner broken down by the hour. So we worked on blocking out pieces of her time to be available to help others. Now, when someone puts pressure on her to commit to something, she can consult her calendar and say, "Sorry, I'm not available that day."

Generosity and service are important, but we all have limits to how much we can give. We just have to discover what those are. Is it always that simple? Of course not. It may take some trial and error and help from God to work on the things within our power to change.

Anthony

Because I'm innately a people pleaser, I didn't do well with the idea of limitations at first. For instance, as I mentioned, my father is well-known, especially in Dallas. I can think of a few instances when I'd be shopping at the NorthPark Foot Locker and random people would come up and wrap me in a hug.

Do I know you? I'd wonder.

I did not. But they knew me because they had come to the church or seen my family on TV, YouTube, or socials. So, even if you desperately need a new pair of shoes because you forgot to pack any, and you only have an hour to catch your plane, you hug them back, take selfies, and chat for a while (even if you're not very good at small talk either).

It's an honor, and I certainly don't mind, but if you are not careful, eventually this will drain you. Well, it drained me. Some people's personalities are better suited for it, but I'm introverted at times. It's easy for things like this to make me feel like I am taking on the weight of the world.

I used to feel guilty about that until Stacy pointed out that due to my need for external validation, I was staying in those scenarios longer than I was able to handle. Some people can talk three hours after the church service is over. I can do that, but then I don't sleep well. If I'm in the middle of touring and going from plane to plane and event to event, I know I'll overextend myself. The next thing I know I will have blown my voice out again.

Stacy also reminded me about the importance of surrounding yourself with people who build you up. You've got to get ready for them, though. My mom used to say, "Dinner's ready. Get your homework off the table and put out the silverware." Mommy was an incredible cook, but there would be times when I got distracted or caught up in something else. She'd just let that good food get cold until I woke up and set the table.

Sometimes you're ready to make good decisions toward health and allow good people and situations to come in your life, but the table isn't set so they can sit down. In the same way, a lot of people complain about finding the right person and meeting good friends. But have you worked on *being* the right person? Have you cleared the junk from the table of your life to make space for the kind of friends who will help you recharge instead of draining your power? You've got to be ready to receive.

Stacy

God doesn't only say, "Set the table"; we must clear the table as well. Sometimes God, or our own awareness, points to people in our lives who we need to get away from. Taking ownership over our lives involves listening to those messages, knowing that it is in our own best interests to take space from those who disrupt our lives.

Anthony

Proverbs 13:20 says, "Walk with the wise and become wise, for a companion of fools suffers harm."

When we walk with those who are wise and kind, there is protection—a sense of things working together for the good. When I had to have vocal surgery in 2017, I didn't have a quick comeback. That muscle had grown weak. But then incredible singers stepped in to help me out, to cover the notes I could no longer hit at the time. Their strengths covered my weakness until I was back at full power again.

In ministry, our goal is for everyone to experience the Spirit and love of God. We receive His power when we come together and admit that we need one another. There's nothing left uncovered in the power of people experiencing God's love.

Stacy

Anthony is one of the most high-energy people I have ever met. I also know that his heart desires to help people. I am sure he would want to hug every last person in that church sanctuary or mall or airport and listen to their stories and pray. But even the most high-capacity cell phone needs to recharge if it is going to continue to function.

That can be a source of guilt for most of us. I imagine it's even more difficult for those in the ministry. I know it is hard for us therapists.

Anthony

Everybody knows what it's like when their phone goes into Low Power Mode. The battery icon turns yellow, you get an alert that your battery is low, and you don't have a choice but to click Accept. To preserve power, all your background apps stop refreshing, and if you don't recharge soon, your phone is going to shut down.

We've all seen those people who are still scrambling to make calls and check their email on 3-percent power. Well, that was me. I always felt like it was my obligation to continue working even when I was going into Low Power Mode.

There's something about faith and ministry. Sometimes in working for God, we forget that He also tells us to rest. We forget about lying down in green pastures. We forget about returning to Him for the restoration of our souls. It's like there's some honor in overworking, like a true Christian is supposed to be miserable, tired, and overloaded. But even God made time to rest during creation on the seventh day (Genesis 2:2).

When I began to figure out the importance of rest, it made my music better and my ideas sharper. My time with people was warm and genuine instead of robotic because I wasn't exhausted and running in Low Power Mode.

I had thought taking time for "self" was selfish. But really, it made me able to give even more.

Stacy

I think if we're all honest with ourselves, we struggle with living out what we've been called to do. But we also struggle at times with being honest with ourselves and, even more, being kind to ourselves. These things are essential if we are to take ownership of ourselves, and they're part of the work we need to do before we're ready to move on.

Anthony

I remember my dad preaching a sermon about Moses, how the old prophet didn't think he was up to the job God was calling him to do. Moses was impulsive, he stuttered, and he had anger issues. But he just kept following the next step that the Lord put in front of him, and God kept working on Moses and used him in a mighty way. He became a leader to the children of Israel and led thousands to freedom (Exodus 2:11–12; 3:1–4:17; Numbers 20:7–12).

Moses lacked conviction, courage, and competence, but God knew it was inside him all along. He just had to get Moses to believe it for himself. That didn't happen overnight. Even though God appeared through pillars of clouds and fire, though He hid Moses in the rock and walked by, though He spoke to His servant like a friend—it still took a long time and a lot of hard work (Exodus 13, 33).

That's Moses' story, but really, you see that same example throughout Scripture time and time again. The Bible is filled with stories of broken, messy humans trying and failing and getting back up to try again. So, if you lack courage, competence, or conviction, look to the Word.

That's my story too. In my lowest points I kept reading Philippians 1 and reminding myself, "He who started a good work in me will be faithful to complete it" (v. 6, my paraphrase). Even when I didn't feel confident or courageous, I kept moving forward by faith. Usually that meant simply taking the next step and doing the next thing God put before me, trusting that no matter how many times I messed everything up, He would still help me to get up and try again.

I can't always see the end result, but God will light that next step. Our purpose and calling is to be confident in the good work God has begun, and then take that next step of faith.

In fact, you might remember that's how I found Stacy. I was so lost, confused, and overcome with doubts and fears that I could no longer see a future. And even though I was the son of a famous preacher, I could not feel God's Spirit around me.

Then I saw a therapist on TV, and the smallest seed of hope stirred up inside. Even though it felt crazy, I allowed that hope to turn to action, reached out, and took that next step that was before me.

Thank God I did.

Stacy

One of the first things Anthony and I talked about once he bravely reached out was the internal voice. One of my fondest memories of my grandmother was her walking around the house talking to herself. "Now where did I put that letter opener?" she would ask, shuffling across the linoleum floor while opening and closing various kitchen drawers.

Grandma would even talk to herself out loud at the store, steering her shopping cart through the produce aisle at Ralphs, muttering, "What should I make for dinner tonight? Hmm, let's see . . ."

My grandmother was also prone to publicly scolding herself by shouting out things like, "I am such a fool!" or "I shouldn't have eaten that—it's too fattening!" She was so immersed in conversation with herself that if someone had replied, she would have been shocked.

"Self-talk" isn't one of those weird, touchy-feely therapy terms. It's something we all do. Whether out loud or only in the mind, we all run a nearly nonstop conversation with ourselves. Self-talk simply refers to the act of communicating with yourself. It is the voice in your head that allows you to contemplate decisions, give yourself advice, and retrieve long-lost memories.

This internal voice serves as your own personal judge, commentator, critic, adviser, supporter, influencer, parent, motivator, and more. Self-talk can be positive or negative, automatic or deliberate. Most importantly, self-talk can be incredibly powerful.

Scientific research and my experience as a psychotherapist both support the opinion that self-talk impacts us in many ways. Negative self-talk can cause stress, anxiety, hopelessness, anger, fear, sadness, and even failure.

I can't do this.

Nobody likes me.

I mess everything up.

I look awful.

Nobody wants to help me.

Some of us seem to be on autopilot when it comes to negative thought patterns. It's as if we switch into a critical or pessimistic state without even realizing it.

A few years back, I had a client who could spin any situation into a negative self-report. If the weather called for rain, she would think, *Well, knowing me, I'll catch a cold.* If a coworker invited her to a party, she would wonder, *Did they just invite me out of pity?* Her knee-jerk reaction was gloom and doubt. As a result, she spent most of her days lost in a fog of deep sadness.

Another client's self-talk was filled with anger and aggression. If traffic was backed up this person would begin to broadcast cynical messages. *These idiots are making me late! Why is the world determined to torture me?*

These poisonous thoughts would linger as she sulked and stomped through her day, ignoring the good and interpreting any small misfortune as confirmation that she was predestined for a life of catastrophe.

On the other hand, positive self-talk can instill hope, create greater happiness, improve well-being, and help build success.

I can handle this.

Everything is going to be all right.

I don't have to be perfect. I only have to do my best.

Early in my career as a therapist, I had a client who was raised by highly critical parents, and as a result she became highly critical of herself. Her self-esteem was so poor and her thoughts so negative that, at thirty-two years old, she could not maintain a job or a relationship for longer than a month.

The criticisms and negativity that we receive as we grow can stick with us as adults. For many of us, we actually pick up that dysfunctional thinking and start negatively talking to ourselves. I worked with my client to engage in more positive self-talk, guiding her to offer compliments and words of encouragement to herself and to stop criticizing so much when she made mistakes. My client did not change overnight. She would sometimes slip back into old behaviors and under that dark cloud of gloom.

But eventually, slowly, she came out of the darkness into the light, and within six months she'd found a job and was dating someone who had possibilities for the future.

That's an example of how significant early-life experiences—a challenging childhood, abuse, or a critical parent—can subconsciously guide us on paths that are destructive and difficult to understand.

All of us have moments when we find ourselves stuck in the rut of negative thoughts and self-talk. The first step is awareness and a desire to pull yourself out of the rut. Here are six simple ways to start:

1. **ASSESS THE ORIGINS.** The history of your negativity will help you manage it from a more compassionate position. Did your mother complain all the time? Was nothing ever good enough for your dad? Were you bullied at school? Think about your history—the events that left a mark. A good start is to question your negative thoughts. *Nothing good ever happens for me.* Is this true or a sad exaggeration? Nothing good? Ever? Where did these thoughts begin? After the divorce? When you moved and had to switch schools in seventh grade? When did you begin to imagine the worst-case scenarios?

2. **INTERRUPT THE NEGATIVE THOUGHTS.** As you realize that your thoughts or words are turning negative, say, "Stop." Say it out loud. Doing this will interrupt your thought process and enable you to pay closer attention to how often negative self-talk occurs as well as the circumstances in which it's happening. Are you more negative in the mornings? At home or at work? Some clients even keep track of how many times a day they find themselves saying, "Stop."

3. **DISTRACT THROUGH ACTION.** Distract yourself from negative thinking by taking action. Walk around the block, empty the dishwasher, bake a cake. Activity often diffuses negative thoughts. Physical action will shift your mind away from rumination and onto the task at hand.

4. **SOFTEN THE BLOW.** If you find yourself in a negative state of mind for legitimate reasons, such as falling back into a bad habit, gaining weight, or making a big mistake, try to soften the impact. If the holidays bring on a few unwanted pounds, instead of thinking, *See? I knew I couldn't do it,* try something a little kinder like, *Okay, I slipped up and gained a few pounds back. I've lost weight before and I can do it again.*

Or let's say you make a mistake at work. Punishing yourself by punching the steering wheel and shouting, "I blew it again! I am *such* an idiot!" might feel like a release in the moment, but ultimately it is not helpful. Be as kind to yourself as you would be to a coworker or friend who made the same error. What would you say to that person? Probably something more along the lines of, "It's okay—nobody gets it right all the time. You'll learn from this and do better in the future."

These shifts do not come without resistance. Don't expect negativity to give up so easily. You may have to wrestle those thoughts before you get the upper hand.

5. **AVOID EXTREMES.** Watch out for terms like *always* and *never.* They create an instant boundary that will keep you from being open to positive thoughts.

   I'll never *get it right.*

   This always *happens to me!*

   Take those negative thoughts to court before they create a sense of doom and steal your hope. We all overreact at times. Maybe it's best to wait until the worst of the storm passes over and to reassess the situation once you have calmed down.

6. **GIVE YOURSELF GRACE.** Shifting from negative to positive takes time. Be patient. Look for progress, not perfection. We can be both the harshest critic and the biggest cheerleader for ourselves.

Take the time to examine your own internal dialogue and listen for clues concerning the roots of your self-doubt, self-loathing, and feelings of inadequacy. We really can help others better when we help ourselves.

STACY'S TIPS TO HELP YOU GET STARTED

- **REFLECTION:** Take time to reflect on whether you've been taking ownership over your life. If you have been, great! If you feel that you haven't been, explore why. Were you raised to believe that you should hand your life's decisions over to another person? (Note: I am not talking about handing things over to God; I am talking about giving ownership over who you are and what you do to a friend, family member, mate, or someone else.) Once you have reflected about who takes ownership of your daily life, it is important to reflect on what you like about your life and what needs to change.

- **REALIZATION:** Many of us do not realize how little we take ownership over our own lives. Here's how this works: if you do not take ownership and responsibility over your own life, you *cannot* create change. Much like if you don't own your car or home, how can you possibly change it? It would be in the hands of someone else to change. You must realize that even if others have hurt you, affected you, or supported you, you are the only one who can truly control your own mind and your heart. You must take charge so you can live a life that is meaningful to you.

- **ACTION:** Get clear about your need to take ownership over your own life.

  - Think about what needs to be changed and identify specific ways you could set about making those changes.
  - As always, find supportive people to keep you motivated, because change can be uncomfortable and support is helpful.

LOOK FOR PROGRESS, NOT PERFECTION.

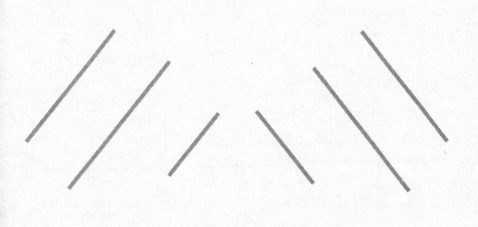

FIVE

FACE YOUR FEAR FACTOR

Do not fear [anything], for I am with you; Do not be
afraid, for I am your God. I will strengthen you, be
assured I will help you; I will certainly take hold of
you with My righteous right hand [a hand of justice, of
power, of victory, of salvation].

ISAIAH 41:10 AMP

Anthony

Up until recently, I had a two-thousand-pound, half-Percheron and half-Thoroughbred horse named Gideon, named after that mighty man of valor from the Old Testament book of Judges. Gideon was one of the great joys of my life, but since it's kind of difficult (and illegal) to ride a horse through downtown Los Angeles, I kept him at a boarding facility in Tyler, Texas.

Since I couldn't be near him full time, I decided I would love on him the best way I could—by bringing him extra food and treats. That's the way to his (and my) heart.

I could go to the pasture and yell, "Gideon!" and even if there were ten other horses out there, his head would come up and he would immediately start thundering toward me. I like to think it's because Gideon's heart was so full of love and happiness that he got excited when he heard my voice, but it was probably more related to the bag of feed that he knew would be accompanying me.

One afternoon as I led Gideon toward the barn he began to prance around like he always did when he knew he was about to get some good treats and loving attention. But this time, just before we made it to the stable door, he planted his feet and began to snort. One second later, with all his strength and weight, he lunged straight toward me! Let me just say that when a one-ton beast is scared and jumps, you get out of the way.

From there Gideon reared up. Suddenly he was twelve feet tall, freaking out, and trying to back away from something that was not obvious to me. I was looking around, trying to figure out what was making my horse so afraid when I realized what was going on. The sun was setting and cast a long shadow on the concrete slab—one that looked like a horse twice the size of Gideon.

My horse did not realize that the threat was only his shadow. He thought that giant black horse was real. In that moment Gideon didn't care about the feed or the brushing or even my love. He was consumed with fear—fear of his own shadow.

Later that night I was driving home, thinking about what had happened. That's when I realized that I had often done the same thing as Gideon. Some areas in my life had cast a huge, scary shadow. But it was only a trick. Actually, it's a trick that has been played on all of us from the beginning of time—a trick between darkness and light. But more about that later.

Stacy

The first video series Anthony and I collaborated on was called "The Power of Perspective." How we see things—our perspectives, our narratives, our belief systems—affects how we feel. If we come upon something that is unfamiliar, like Gideon seeing his shadow for the first time, it can be completely frightening. Anxiety and fear can lead to a knee-jerk trauma response that causes us to lash out, flee, or freeze, unintentionally affecting others or ourselves.

It's important to investigate something new that causes an excessive emotional response, and part of this book's mission is to help with that—because that's where faith meets therapy. Again, for some, there is a stigma associated with therapy, especially among certain communities of faith. There's also a stigma about introspection, which often stems from an underlying fear of "the dark," those unexplored parts of our personalities. Those stigmas might be part of the reason we can get so secretly sick and consumed with fears.

Anthony

Gideon was a powerful animal. When he got spooked and began to thrash around, I was in danger. I could have been seriously injured, even killed. He also could have hurt himself.

Time and time again, when I have been afraid, Stacy has reminded me, "Anthony, you need to understand how powerful you are." What does she mean by that? She doesn't want me to unintentionally hurt myself or someone else who might be nearby.

God has given all of us power that manifests itself in different ways and in different places, but, as the famous quote from *Spider-Man* goes, "With great power comes great responsibility."[1] We can use that power to harm or to heal.

Because shadows usually appear larger than life, if we don't have a clear understanding that our shadows cannot harm us, we start responding to them like they are real threats. That response causes us to lose sight of those around us, and our actions often hurt those who are closest to us.

The equivalent of "fear not" is commanded in the Bible more than three hundred times.[2] Why do you think that is? I believe it is because we need to be reminded of the magnitude of dysfunction that can occur if we allow fear to manifest itself in us. When we operate from a spirit of fear, it drains our power and conflicts with God's call for our lives. In fear, we are a danger to ourselves and to others.

Fear is definitely not where God wants us to be.

Stacy

Gideon was a powerful animal, and we are powerful people. Fear that is understood and addressed can only serve to help us feel even more powerful. Actually, understanding and managing *any* of our feelings is a way to feel more in control of our emotions and overall life.

What I find interesting, though, is that unharnessed power can make us feel helpless, which only serves to magnify anxiety and fear. Allowing ourselves to do this important work, while having faith that we are not alone and God is walking with us, is an important path to healing and growth.

Anthony

That is so true. As a leader in ministry, I have power and responsibility. A therapist carries great power and responsibility. But we all have influence over someone, which means the power and responsibility thing is for all of us.

The Bible is clear that God has given us all a certain amount of power and responsibility.

Second Timothy 1:7 says, "God gave us a spirit not of fear but of power and love and self-control" (ESV). I take that to mean that love and self-control harness power. Our full potential, as related to our unique power, cannot operate properly when fear is at play. Perfect love for God, ourselves, and others casts out that fear (1 John 4:18).

Stacy

Everybody experiences fear, even those who appear to be incredibly brave.

Strangely enough, fear can be a great motivator. Fear of financial problems can motivate us to manage our money better. Fear of losing a loved one can inspire us to maximize the time we spend with them. Whatever has caused your fear, it is important to know that fear is a signal to you, a sign to stop and see what's going on so you can handle the situation thoughtfully instead of reactively.

So fear can be a good thing. It can save us. It can keep us from falling off a cliff, help us not to embarrass ourselves, keep us away from dangerous people or things.

I have a friend who, for a while, was living off junk food and sugary snacks. Finally her doctor dropped the bomb: "If you keep eating like this you will end up with diabetes." It must have been the right message at the right time because he scared her straight. Now she's eating superfoods and grass-fed beef and getting onto me when I eat junk!

The fear of poverty could inspire someone to work harder and save. Fear of failing a test might drive you to study more. Fear can be a healthy stimulus.

In this section of the book, we are discussing problematic fears and anxieties. Whenever we feel threatened physically, emotionally, spiritually, or financially, our brains tell our bodies to kick into the fear response. This is often thought of as fight-or-flight, but we can't forget the other possible reactions as well: freeze or fawn.

If a bully attacks, whether it's a physical or verbal threat, fighting or fleeing are not the only reactions you might experience. You could also freeze, paralyzed by the fear of being physically harmed. The fawning response is people-pleasing, placating, saying or doing whatever it takes to neutralize the threat. Most of us have experienced that response, whether it was with a parent, boss, or mate.

There are healthy and unhealthy versions of all those responses. Sometimes you could potentially cycle through all four. If someone threatens your life while you are walking down the street, first you might freeze while trying to figure out whether it's better to run or fight back. You might even start fawning.

"You look like a really nice person," you could assure them. "Please, take my purse. It's genuine Kate Spade from the outlet, not a knockoff. Totally matches your eyes. Do you need an iPhone?"

The fearful experience that I just mentioned is one of physical danger, but sometimes emotional fears trigger these responses as well.

Anthony

One of my biggest fears used to be disappointing people and losing them from my life. Maybe you could say it's a fear of being alone. That mindset can turn you into a codependent people pleaser at the expense of your own well-being. If I hold you accountable, you might leave, so instead I'll lower my standards and work hard enough for both of us.

Over time, that fear turned into a full-blown anxiety. I constantly worried about the status of my relationships, overanalyzing every little thing I said and did.

Stacy

Often our past experiences or past traumas create or add to a fear. The fearful thing is not currently happening, but we fear what *could* happen again. An example would be if you misjudged someone or lost your temper and it cost you an important relationship. So you bite your tongue and turn to people-pleasing in the next relationship, obsessing over not making that mistake again. Or if you had a relationship with someone who cheated on you, you might worry that your next partner will cheat on you too.

Fear tends to dissipate when whatever we are afraid of goes away, but anxiety is a lingering feeling that sometimes stays for a long period of time. Anxiety comes from the worries we are thinking about in our minds. And any of you who are overthinkers can count on the fact that your overthinking can create anxiety. Anxiety intensified can make us engage in these fight, flight, freeze, and fawn triggers as well.

It is exhausting to live in a constant state of anxiety. It repeats, builds, and becomes a vicious cycle. A person can eventually become anxious about their own anxiety.

Therapists are no different. Many people who know me or who have seen me on TV are surprised to find out that I am actually quite shy. I was that kid who hid behind her mother's leg on a regular basis. As a result, as a young adult, when I was in certain settings, I would be afraid of what to do if someone I didn't know started to talk with me. That fear would create anxiety even before I entered a room full of people! Ultimately I realized that I had to confront that fear, analyze it, and begin to work on having more courage in that area. I started creating a mental list of things to talk about—my new favorite TV show or even the weather—before I walked into places that triggered my shyness.

As I started to get more comfortable, I realized that I needed to use my strengths to overcome my weakness—and it hit me: I talk to people for a living. So I simply began engaging those I was with by asking them for stories about their lives, and I discovered we were both more comfortable.

A funny thing came out of these efforts. I was talking with a famous comedienne at a party, asking her about her life, and she said, "Stacy, you can't help yourself. You wear your therapist hat everywhere you go. And for those of us who want to tell our stories, you are the best guest around!"

Anthony

Stacy's story reminds me of a story about my dad. No one would guess this, but my dad had a speech impediment growing up. Studies show that speaking in public is most people's number one fear,[3] so you can imagine how anxious he was about that. When I was about six years old, I remember being in his office. He had these jaw exercisers in his desk drawer and would spend time every day working to improve his speech.

He didn't just back down to that fear and let it control him or stop his calling. Dad worked hard to overcome it, and now he's viewed as one of Christianity's greatest orators, speaking on radio and TV around the world.

Stacy

That's a good example of how fear can be a motivator, using your strength to overcome a weakness. What a great role model.

Anthony

Dad uses another story in his sermons to illustrate fear. A pilot was flying over the Rocky Mountains and found himself in a dense fog. The plane was surrounded by haze, and the pilot had zero visibility. Even though it was a very scary situation, he continued to travel over the mountains at five hundred miles per hour, full speed ahead.

How? Because he could trust his gauges.

God has given us His Word as a gauge for when the way seems dark and fear takes over. Sometimes we can't trust our vision. But we can always trust God's Word.

He also sends His light through people to help guide us in dark times. He gives us mentors, pastors, therapists, trusted friends. That's another reason a good support system is so important.

Stacy

In times of fear it is best to return to those trusted supporters. Go back to the light of your faith and the guidance you know is safe.

Anthony

That's why I stay in therapy. I keep close to my family and stay active with friends, even when I am feeling depressed and want to stay home by myself. Flying solo will make you much more likely to crash. You can't wait for disaster to strike. It's usually too late by then.

Philippians 4:6 tells us to be anxious for nothing. Again, that's a tough one for me. There have been times in life when it seems I felt anxious about *every*thing. The rest of the verse says that we should approach every situation with prayer and thanksgiving. That's all I can do—stay in the present moment, give thanks, and honestly and humbly pray, *You know what, God? I'm having a really hard time today. I need Your help to move away from the darkness of fear and find peace. Please show me the next step I need to take to move toward this.*

Stacy

Fear puts our focus on the future or past. That's why it is important to reorient to the present moment and take it one step at a time. Your mind can't think two things at the same time. If you force your mind to focus on something else, fear cannot coexist with whatever else you've got going on. It could be emptying the dishwasher, talking to a friend, cleaning the bathroom, or reading scriptures about overcoming fear.

Anthony

Romans 12:2 says to be transformed by the renewing of your mind so you can test and prove what is the good, pleasing, and perfect will of God. Renewing my mind has been a huge part of change for me. Not just positive self-talk but encouraging myself with the Word of God and striving to believe what He has said about me in those moments, even if I struggle to believe it for myself.

One of my mom's favorite songs of mine was "Fighting for Us." I held her hand and sang that chorus into her ear as she was taking her last breath. The next day I had to get on a plane to England to sing at an event because Mommy insisted that ministry carry on, and I promised her it would. We all did what she asked.

I won't lie and tell you that I did not feel fear in those moments. But I would look to the gauge of God's Word. Deuteronomy 3:22 promises, "Do not fear . . . for the LORD your God is the One fighting for you" (NASB).

It was a new level of faith for me. But as I stood on that platform to sing, barely twenty-four hours after my mother had passed away, I felt God's love and His peace. I did not feel fear.

I knew He was fighting for me.

——— STACY'S TIPS TO HELP YOU GET STARTED

- **REFLECTION:** It's important to dig down deep and identify not only your fears but also their source. For instance, saying, *I am afraid of snakes* is not enough. Get very specific about what you fear. Is it the snake's bite? The venom? Just the sight of a snake slithering or the feeling of the scales against your skin? Then ask yourself how you developed these fears. Did you have a bad experience with snakes early on? Were you frightened by one? Did a family member or friend get badly bitten? Did you see a disturbing film or TV show as a child? Be as detailed as possible.
- **REALIZATION:** Once you have identified your fears and examined the sources, it's important to also question them. Assess them in the light of facts. Let's switch from snakes to Disneyland so I can give you an illustration. The Haunted Mansion has an elaborate display of ghosts and goblins, but it's more cartoonish than scary. I took my daughter and her friend Tasha to the mansion when they were ten. As we approached it, Tasha began to tremble and cry.

"I'm scared of going on this ride," she confessed. We sat on a park bench and talked about it.

"Have you ever been to the Haunted Mansion?" I asked.

"No," Tasha said. "But my mom says when she was four, she rode it and cried and screamed all the way through, so I'm scared of what's in there too."

"Well, your mom was four years old," I replied. "You're ten. Are you afraid of all the same things your mom is?"

"No," she admitted.

"Come on, then," I said. "Let's give it a try." We waited in line, rode the stretchy elevator down and queued up to climb into the Doom Buggy. Tasha was trying to be brave, but tears were streaming down her face, and I'm sure, in that moment, the other Disney guests thought, *Who is this cruel woman forcing a crying child to go through the Haunted Mansion?* (It's okay, I'm a therapist . . .) We twisted through the dimly lit mansion while ghosts waltzed, lightning struck, and singing skeletons appeared between us in the car. When it was all over, Tasha bounced out of the buggy with a huge smile. "I did it! I did it!" she exclaimed. "And I wasn't scared! Can we go on it again?"

It's important to notice when your fears impair your level of functioning. The fear of heights is rational. High places can be dangerous, and they require caution. But if your fear of heights has put you in a place where you can't drive across a bridge, it's impacting your ability to function. For that reason it's important to investigate the things that make us afraid. If it's only your "shadow," find the courage you need to press on.

- **ACTION**: Learn to differentiate between fears and realities.

  - Commit to not letting your fears get in the way of what is important in your life, but also be kind to yourself.
  - Set goals both large and small. Break goals down into bite-sized steps. If you are trying to overcome a

debilitating fear of heights, you don't need to schedule a skydive right away. Start with something smaller.

- Then, finally, encourage yourself. Again, you are the only person who is with you 24 hours a day, 7 days a week, 365 days a year. Don't tear yourself down or be your own worst critic.

SOMETIMES WE CAN'T TRUST OUR VISION. BUT WE CAN ALWAYS TRUST GOD'S WORD.

SIX

UNDERSTAND THE PROBLEMS AND PURPOSES OF ANGER

He who is slow to anger has great understanding [and profits from his self-control], but he who is quick-tempered exposes and exalts his foolishness [for all to see].

PROVERBS 14:29 AMP

Anthony

Confession: I have a problem controlling my temper.

When I was a little kid, my dad would look at me, shake his head, and ask, "Son, *why* do you get so frustrated?"

All I could do was shrug. I had no clue what caused my fuse to be so short. I tried to control it, but I didn't really have the tools, so I went from being a frustrated kid to a frustrated adult who is easily triggered by not feeling valued, by being dismissed, or worst of all, by feeling emasculated.

One day in a therapy session, Stacy told me to think about what God would say and feel about my anger. Verses 19 and 20 of James chapter 1 came to mind. It says, "Let everyone be a cautious and thoughtful listener, a speaker of carefully chosen words and slow to anger, because human anger does not produce the righteousness of God" (my paraphrase).

I have experienced the truth of those verses firsthand. Anger was not producing the righteousness that God desired for my life.

In the past couple of years, with the loss of my mom and so many others in my family, my sadness has sometimes come out in the form of anger. It is an easier emotion to show than some of the others. A lot of times, for me, it's actually sadness that wants to disguise itself.

Sometimes in sessions Stacy will catch a certain look in my eyes and she'll say, "Wait. Hold on. What was that?" What she was seeing was sadness trying to show itself, except I was stuffing it down before it could. Sometimes we would sit in silence for a few moments because she did not want me to move until I addressed what she sensed and saw.

That's how therapy works. Those things that make you feel the most uncomfortable? Those are the ones your therapist will insist that you discuss.

When the Bible says, "Be slow to anger," to me, that also means, "Be quick to find out and deal with what you are really feeling inside." Anger is usually a cover for something deeper going on under the surface.

As I mentioned, anger is a safer emotion for most of us because it doesn't make you feel vulnerable or weak. The only way I've been able to deal with my anger problem is to obey God's Word in James 1:19 as mentioned above, to be quick to listen and slow to speak. In other words, *Stop talking, Anthony. You don't have to let everybody know how you feel about everything. Two ears, one mouth. Try to listen twice as much as you speak.*

I love my siblings so much. All of them know about my temper, and there are times they can sense me winding up internally even before I say a word. Priscilla will tap my leg or simply put her hand where I can see it to tell me in sibling code, *Don't talk yet.* In some cases she will whisper, "I got this." Priscilla, Chrystal, and Jonathan are so aware of me and my heart that they are constantly helping me with my struggles. It's so important to have people in your life who know your weaknesses and will join you in your journey toward maturity.

James 1:19 is a verse that would change the world right now if people would pay attention. There is so much anger everywhere. Can you imagine if people leaned into accountability, quit talking so much, and started listening to one another instead?

Stacy

Anthony doesn't just talk about the principles and theories. He's not just passing out advice. He is quick to say, "This is me. I'm talking about myself here. I struggle with this problem too."

The truth is that we all have struggles like these. I have had them as well. I have lots of skills and training and tools to manage emotional distress, and yet even I, Stacy Kaiser—a therapist—see a therapist sometimes. And as a college professor at California State University, Northridge, who is teaching future therapists, I encourage my students to have their own therapy sessions as well. As a matter of fact, the university requires it; we all need an objective listener and new coping strategies in times of stress. Even in times of joy it's nice to have an extra cheerleader to acknowledge the good times.

We've all wrestled with the balance of controlling our anger and not being so passive that others walk all over us. It can be tough, even for mental health professionals.

In our current culture, unbridled anger is a glamorized and socially acceptable emotion—even more these days when everyone seems to want to prove their point through outrage. Reality TV, for example, rewards the idea of flipping out on people. Drama will give you more screen time. Be anything but boring. Crying and sadness are seen as weaknesses while anger is viewed as strength.

Social media rewards anger and outrage by drawing attention to fireworks while offering a perfect platform for passive-aggressive attacks.

Listen—anger is not the problem. Anger is how our emotions let us know something is wrong. If your temper is destructive, out of control, harmful to others, or creating problems with your job and relationships, that has crossed over into an anger issue.

But anger, in its right place, can get things done.

Anthony

Righteous anger, yes. The Bible doesn't say, "Don't be angry"; it tells us not to rush into it (Ecclesiastes 7:9). The Bible also tells us that it's okay to be angry but not to sin (Ephesians 4:26). We also should not let anger control our emotions because emotions left to themselves don't have intellect.

When I was a contestant on *The Voice*, the mentor who was my coach was the singer Jewel. I was talking about being an emotional person, and she said, "Anthony, what you have to understand is that righteous anger brings about righteous change."

I never forgot those words. When the Bible tells us to be slow to become angry, I think that means we don't rush into judgment. It's not an emotional response. We give it careful thought first, thinking about what role we might have played in the situation, considering the other person's point of view.

Mother Teresa, Gandhi, Martin Luther King Jr., Jesus—they all achieved things through righteous anger. Jesus made a whip and turned over tables in church (John 2:15)! Righteous anger brought about a righteous change.

Stacy

I want to talk about the difference between reacting versus responding. *Reacting* is being quick to get angry. It's a knee-jerk response, throwing things out into the world with no filter or control. But *responding* is exactly what that Bible verse is talking about. It's taking your time and being thoughtful. Whatever is bothering you can be talked about in a way that is healthy, productive, and will accomplish something positive.

One of the biggest problems I encounter with people in relationships, whether it's intimate relationships, friendships, or family relationships, is that people are quick to get angry.

Anthony has gained a lot of hard-won knowledge and experience with this and has developed a great understanding of reacting versus responding.

Anthony

What I can say from experience is that *reacting* is giving the power of the narrative away; *responding* is retaining it. This is nothing like staying calm when someone or something is trying to push you toward a reaction.

For example, I am bad about building a case against someone without first having all the proven facts—as opposed to the ones I've made up in my head. I'm capable of jumping to conclusions and making someone out to be the villain. The biggest consequence for me is, after I create that story line, I stew on it and then blow up at the first opportunity. The result is always me saying hurtful things. Then, later, I think about my delivery and what I said, and I have to apologize after the damage is done.

Let's say I feel like someone is taking advantage of my mom and dad's life's work, legacy, time, or platform. I am quick to want to defend them. I believe this is righteous anger. But when I rush to speak, it doesn't help the situation if I attack that person or say immature and hurtful things. It's not fair, and I know it.

I have a hard time settling myself down in the moment. I've offended people I work with and people who work with my family. It's part of my protective nature, coupled with my sensitivity, but that's no excuse for making messes.

Stacy

It bears repeating: what you think impacts how you feel. If you process someone's behavior as, *Wow, my father has this amazing gift, so it's natural that people are going to want his attention and time in his light,* then those thoughts will make you feel grateful, happy, and at peace.

On the other hand, if you look at the situation like, *Everyone is bothering my dad because they just want something from him,* you will feel angry and frustrated and look for ways to fix it. This all plays into reacting versus responding.

Now, in truth, most people probably just want to connect with Anthony's dad because he is wise and inspirational. There probably are also a few bad apples in the bunch who actually are trying to take advantage. It would be natural to be angry with those types, but it's not the feeling of anger that is the issue; it's how you deal with it and what it does inside and outside of you.

Anthony

It reminds me of something I heard Bruce Wilkinson say once. He wrote *The Prayer of Jabez,* which was huge in the early 2000s. Bruce came to our home church to speak and during a talk said, "If you were wearing a sweatshirt and I walked up, slapped you on the shoulder, and said, 'Hey, what's up?' that would be a friendly greeting, right? But let's say you had a cut on your shoulder. You would probably pull back and shoot me an angry look. Do you really have the right to be mad? I wasn't aware that you were injured under your shirt."

That story stuck with me because we often don't have a clue what injuries lie beneath the surface. The way we move from reacting to responding is to work on our own healing, letting people know where we are hurt and what we are going through.

That was my story. I was covering up old injuries and then reacting with anger when someone would accidently hit that spot and hurt me. But how could they know?

First, I had to work on getting myself better.

Stacy

We have a tendency to blame anger on others and forces outside of our control, but it goes back to working on the things within our power to change—our own attitudes and responses. Crucial to that process is knowing yourself and your own triggers.

For example, Anthony and I have discussed the fact that we both have a pet peeve about people being on time. If we realize that about ourselves, we are left with some choices. If a friend shows up late for a meeting, we might react with thoughts such as, *This is so disrespectful! They don't care about my time. I'm not going to put up with this anymore.*

But if, instead, we respond first in a way that considers that we are sticklers for being on time and we don't jump to conclusions, we could take a deep breath and calmly say something like, "I love being on time. It's a value and priority for me because I have a very tight schedule. I enjoy spending time with you, but I need us to work together a bit better. If you are going to be late, would you please let me know with plenty of time in advance?"

Anthony

Thinking through responses is something I now treasure. Although I am still working on it, it helps me avoid so much irreparable damage. It's so much easier on the back end if you're proactive and thoughtful up front.

Speaking of proactive, by now you know I love houses. So much that I recently got my real estate license just so I can look at places for sale without a Realtor. You can tell when a house was quickly slapped together without much of a plan. We have a lot of those in California. Some of them are truly beautiful from the curb, but eventually they start to crumble. If an earthquake hits a ten-million-dollar home in the hills with a crack running down the wall, no matter how small it is, the crack could instantly become a massive problem.

In the same way, we need a plan to deal with anger, because if we react too quickly out of raw emotion, it will all start to come down—friendships, careers, relationships.

Therapy is part of my plan, a solid investment. I think of Stacy as my emotional architect, preemptively giving me a logical blueprint for how to structure my responses.

Stacy

One problem with anger is that we might have a plan, but someone or something throws it out of whack. It helps to learn the warning signs.

I picture an anger elevator shooting to the top of a tall building. When my anger starts to rise, my heart starts pounding and my face feels hot. We all have those first warning signs when our tempers are about to boil over. That's a sign to slow down, breathe, and wait until the elevator gets to a lower floor.

Anthony

What are some ways to keep our anger under control?

Stacy

I try to step back mentally, emotionally, and even physically, if needed. My family will tell you that I am notorious for leaving the room to calm down. My bedroom is my peaceful sanctuary, and I will go there if I can. If I am out of the house, I might excuse myself to go to the restroom or head to my car or take a walk. Once away, I will take some deep breaths and give myself a time-out to process events and circumstances. Sometimes that means I'll have to tell someone, "Okay, hang on. I need some space right now to figure this out."

It can also help to vent it to a trusted friend and get an objective point of view. Just the process of getting it out of your head and saying it out loud is often beneficial for gaining perspective.

Anthony

I was at the boxing gym the other day and the trainer, Jack, said something insulting as a joke. This other guy took a swing at him, just kidding around, not really trying to connect. Thing is, Jack leaned in at the same time and took a full-on uppercut to the jaw.

Suddenly everything got quiet and tense. *Uh-oh*, I thought. *This could go really, really bad.*

We all waited, watching. Jack took a deep breath before turning and storming out of the gym. He must have paced the parking lot for at least thirty minutes trying to cool down. Bottom line, they worked it out. I watched that clash from the sidelines thinking about how he kept his cool and didn't just instantly react, because if he had, it would have been a huge brawl. But Jack has preemptively done the work, so his reflex was to walk away and cool down. He has no idea how much I admired his strength in that moment.

James 1:22 says it's not enough to just hear God's Word; we must put it into practice.

Stacy

You can usually tell how angry someone is by how much space it takes them to calm down. Two minutes, no big deal. Thirty minutes means Jack must have been really upset. As with anything we are trying to improve, practice becomes habit.

Another tip: if you are on the other end of a clash, don't chase after that angry person. Give them some time and space. You can talk it out further when things are calm.

Focusing on some level of relaxation is a good way to get through anger. You can't be relaxed and angry at the same time. It's physically impossible. Take a long walk. Light candles. Make a sandwich. Listen to music. Have a playlist ready just for when your mood needs a music break.

Anthony

The truth is, flipping out is only an illusion of strength. It takes real strength to keep your anger under control.

Psalm 37:8 says, "Refrain from anger and turn from wrath; do not fret—it leads only to evil." Reactive anger only leads toward bad things. It's not righteous.

Stacy

I have a cousin who will say, "God help me" when she gets angry. If her sister is in the room she will reply with, "God's not going to help you with this one. You're going to have to help yourself."

The question is, does God take anger away, or is that our responsibility?

Anthony

When we experience extreme emotions like grief, anger, sadness, or fear, I believe it's about being honest, allowing yourself to feel those things, and then handing them over to God. You've done the best you can do, so you can trust God to help with the rest.

During this conversation, I have been both convicted and reminded to trust and look to God more and more with controlling my anger. I'm not where I should be yet. I've still got some work to do, and for me, it starts with believing what God says.

Ecclesiastes 7:9 says, "Do not be quickly provoked in your spirit, for anger resides in the lap of fools." Sometimes I have to repeat that over and over and let the Word work its way into my heart.

Proverbs 29:11 says, "Fools give full vent to their rage, but the wise bring calm in the end."

If I want to be wise and not foolish, that means I need to step up and control myself. I want to be a peacemaker, the kind of person who brings calm to a situation, not chaos and rage.

Stacy

It's one thing to think about controlling our own anger, but what do we do when someone else is angry with us?

Anthony

Some people are trying to push your buttons. They want to bring you to their level of anger. But as people of faith, we are called to rise above it. Like Stacy mentioned, give them space and don't jump to any conclusions. Respond rather than react, and work toward talking it out in the calmest, most honest way possible.

If someone has done you wrong or is your flat-out enemy, Proverbs 25:2-22 says to be nice to them and in doing this you'll "heap burning coals . . . on their heads" (NLT). Sounds extreme, but I've experienced this firsthand. If you can find it within yourself to be kind, in spite of the issue, it will, in most cases, lead to the other party having moments of deep thought that lead them to concluding that they were wrong—without you having to defend yourself or try to convince them to calm down. Your thoughtful actions will speak volumes for you.

Stacy

Never in the history of anger has a person been calmed down by being yelled at or told to calm down. Typically love, compassion, and kindness will help, but we ultimately cannot control other people. If you lead with kindness and fail, don't take it too personally.

Anthony

It also helps me to remember what God has done for me. For instance, on the cross Jesus had every right to react in anger and literally stop everything. Instead, He decided to show us the definition of mercy and grace held together by an elaborate display of perseverance and patience. He knew that although His ordeal would be horrifically painful, the outcome would be worth it. That should make us all want to be more patient and merciful to others.

There is a part of anger that's self-righteous—it assumes that we are right and someone else is wrong. The Bible says we all mess up. We all are selfish. Revenge and retaliation belong to the Lord. Romans 12:19 says, "Do not take revenge, my dear friends, but leave room for God's wrath, for it is written: 'It is mine to avenge; I will repay,' says the Lord."

I do not want to take what belongs to God.

A lot of times, my anger comes from my desire to control things. If I trust God the way I say I do, then control belongs to Him too.

——— STACY'S TIPS TO HELP YOU GET STARTED

- **REFLECTION:** It is important to get to know your own anger. Where does it come from? What did you learn about anger from your childhood and recent past? What triggers your anger? What do you need to do to calm your anger? When is your anger valid, and when is it unreasonable?
- **REALIZATION:** The above information is important, but it is also important to realize the impact your anger has had on others and yourself. How has your anger gotten in the way? How has it hurt

you? Others? What negative feelings do you typically have once you have unleashed your anger? How do you hope to grow?

- **ACTION**: Don't just leave it there. Do something constructive.

  - Come up with an anger-management plan. Use the techniques we have suggested in this chapter or think of your own. Note: an anger-management plan should never include physical violence toward another person. If you'd like to buy a punching bag, that is okay.
  - Heal any past wounds that have created or added to your anger.

RIGHTEOUS ANGER BRINGS ABOUT A RIGHTEOUS CHANGE.

SEVEN

FIND GRACE FOR GUILT AND SHAME

Where sin increased, God's grace increased much more.

ROMANS 5:20 GNT

Anthony

Growing up as the namesake of Dr. Tony Evans was hard sometimes. I saw how much my dad loved studying and school and teaching, and I grew more and more overwhelmed with the expectations I put on myself. I did not believe that I could measure up, but still, I would try to convince myself that someday I could figure out how to get a doctorate like my dad and love all the same things he does and carry on the legacy he has built.

Eventually I realized that although we share the same name, God did not build me the same way. In reality we are opposite in many ways.

I'm a creative daydreamer who feels deeply and overthinks things and communicates through songs. Being a creative soul was not cool in my school. I tried fitting in and being something I was not, but it only produced a ton of guilt and shame, and that load just kept getting heavier as time passed.

It took a lot of work and a lot of years to overcome that shame. In many ways I am still working. But that process led to a career in music, albums I have made, concerts, worship sessions. That work led to this book that you are holding right now. I would have missed so many blessings without the work.

Stacy

Shame means different things to different people, but we are not referring to feelings of embarrassment or guilt. Guilt can help us understand how our choices and actions affect others; it typically occurs when we have done something wrong or think we have. Shame is bigger and more internally focused. Shame is when we actually feel like there is something wrong with us. It goes beyond *doing* something wrong and says, *I am wrong; I am bad.*

Shame is a universal emotion—something we all have dealt with at some time or another. We can experience shame in some religious settings. Shame is a feeling that can make us feel stuck and unworthy, and it can make us avoid going to places that usually lift us up.

Anthony

Most of us who have grown up in a community of faith have wrestled with an unhealthy level of shame. We come together in groups and talk about standards, but then we go home and wrestle with our performance alone, wondering why we do not and cannot seem to measure up.

Private shame will make you a great pretender. You act like you are doing fine, but you're not. That creates more secrecy and shame.

Stacy

I should add that there are times when it is appropriate to feel shame, but we should not allow ourselves to get stuck in it for too long. I recently worked with a woman who stole from a supermarket to feed her children. She got caught and almost went to jail. Can you imagine a more difficult situation than having hungry children and no money for food? And yet you might be put in jail and taken away from the very children you were trying to take care of.

This woman felt horrible about the choices she had made, so we talked about alternative options—how she could have gone to a food bank or found other resources rather than stealing. The important thing is to reflect on what you've done wrong, make a commitment to do better, and make amends the best you can.

We want to talk here about unhealthy shame. That's what most of us get stuck in. It is when we place condemnation upon ourselves in a way that is not deserved, healthy, or productive. A lot of people fall into shame if they fail at a job or relationship. They will torture themselves endlessly, fixating on the question, *What is wrong with me?*

Maybe what's wrong with you is what is wrong with us all: You are human. Humans fall short. We make mistakes. We sometimes make decisions that we think are for the best in the moment (like the woman who stole for her children instead of trying to find other ways to get help). Giving yourself permission to be human is not always easy.

Anthony

We all have to make a decision: Am I going to move toward hope and use this scenario to be better, or am I going to use it as an excuse to give up? In the moment of frustration and disgust, quitting feels good.

We all struggle to believe we are worth the path of hope because the "being human" package includes our drive to measure up, which pushes us toward perfectionism. Attempting to be perfect puts us under a lot of pressure. It's often easier to just give up. But that only causes more shame down the road.

Stacy

Constant pressure and feeling like you may not reach the bar that has been set creates a greenhouse for shame to grow wild. There is a fine line between trying to meet standards and pushing yourself into a place where shame makes it nearly impossible to get anything done.

In therapy sessions I often hear people focusing on their failures, beating themselves down because they "haven't done right"—right by God's standards, by their own, by their friend's, or family's, or significant other's. I see a lot of clients who are carrying a heavy load of shame. The load is so impossible to carry that they seek help, and rightly so.

The opposite of shame is grace—receiving God's grace, offering it, giving grace to yourself for the mistakes you have made.

Anthony

Before Stacy and I sat down to write this, I was walking all around my house, adjusting pictures an inch or two and nudging the books and candles on my coffee table so everything looked exactly in place. Maybe obsessing over details is a way to manage my anxiety, because I do that with my life too. I keep trying to reposition myself, nudging and pushing and trying to get things "just right." When I am successful in that, I feel satisfied; and when I am not, it can put me right into a spiral of shame.

Let me explain. Unrealistic expectations and perfectionism set the standard within my career, relationships, emotions, and physical and spiritual life. But it can also be a source of constant shame and guilt, because I will never get all my ducks in a row. Life is never going to be perfect. Things are always going to be slightly off and sometimes simply falling apart.

Stacy had to work with me a lot concerning the balance between perfection and grace. I'm still working on it. I can't get that perfect either.

Stacy

No one is perfect, and there's no shame in that—ha!

Anthony

Oh, you gotta laugh. Sometimes the most graceful thing you can do is laugh at yourself and keep going.

If I am doing a performance, I strive for excellence. But sometimes I hit a bad note. I go flat or sharp or come in too early; occasionally I will forget the words. I've hit a lot of bad notes in my music career. But if I would have given up because I got stuck in shame, I would've missed out on so much opportunity and blessing. I had to learn the art of "autocorrecting" as I continue to sing. There have been times when I was leading worship for thousands and the big emotional moment in the song came, and I belted out a sour note. When something like that happens, I cannot camp there and let it get in my head. I've got to lean in to my experience and make a correction as I continue to move on. The band is not going to stop and let me do it over again until it's pitch-perfect. We'd get stuck in the verse and never make it to the chorus. That's not how live performances work, and that's not how real life works either.

We are going to hit some bad notes now and then. But you must learn from your mistakes, make corrections as you go forward, and keep moving on.

Stacy

Pursuing excellence is a good quality, right? God has put Anthony on the public stage and Anthony wants to give his very best. But perfection is a myth for human beings, and striving for it can cause a lot of us guilt and shame. Work hard. Try your best. Maintain reasonable expectations.

Anthony

Amen. Say that one more time for the people in the back, please.

Stacy

Shame sabotages grace. The goal is to strike a balance between being aware of who you are and what you are doing while having grace when you stumble along the way.

Anthony

I've come to a place where I value authenticity. If I am constantly monitoring my behavior, being hard on myself, or striving for perfection, my quality of life deteriorates, and I end up unhappy. Being authentic is what drives me out of a place of shame. Music is a good example. People will connect with authentic passion over perfection any day.

Stacy

Another path out of shame is to remember that the world isn't as focused on your faults as you are. People generally walk around with good intentions, eager to give the benefit of the doubt. If the people in your life are hyperfocused on your faults, it may be time to reevaluate your relationships. We will talk more about that in the chapters about toxic people.

Anthony

A balanced perspective can come from good support. God sends others to speak truth into our lives because it can be so difficult to see things for what they are. Ephesians 4:15 says we should speak the truth in love. I think that means we care enough to be honest because we want the best for our loved ones and friends. But honesty is not an excuse to be harsh or controlling or to tear somebody down. We're supposed to encourage one another and build one another up. Sometimes that means we have to go to a friend and say, "Hey, don't you think you're being too hard on yourself?"

When you set expectations too high, you are setting yourself up to fail. Failure fuels shame, and sometimes our response is to say, "Oh well, I'm just not going to have any standards then. What's the use?"

Shame feels terrible, so the pendulum swings too far the other way. No standards, no shame. But that doesn't work either, so you get stuck in the extremes of setting standards too low or too high.

I think that's why so many of us feel stuck. Shame is like a freezer. It keeps you from moving, from action or change. I've got some mystery leftovers that have been stuck in my freezer for more than a year now. They're covered in so much frost that I can't even tell what they used to be anymore. But instead of cleaning out my freezer, I leave that door shut and let them just pile up, hidden, out of sight. Gross, right?

Stacy

I describe shame as a cold, wet blanket. You don't even want to get out of bed; you just hide under the covers and make the world go away. Even though that blanket is cold and wet, you still see it as a source of comfort.

People who live in shame struggle with anger and relationship issues. A lot of addictions can be linked to shame. If you feel terrible about yourself, alcohol or pills or food or porn or social media can be a great place to hide out. At first. But then the vicious cycle begins, and it only drags you farther down into the pit.

Scripture tells us to bring it into the light (Ephesians 5:12–13). That means we talk about our shame instead of trying to cover it up. We risk being vulnerable and stop hiding. We work toward healthy expectations of self and others.

Shame hinders success. What can you truly accomplish if you feel horrible about yourself?

Anthony

Romans 3:23 reminds us that all have sinned and fallen short of God's glory, but Psalm 25:3 says, "No one who hopes in you will ever be put to shame." And Romans 8:1 tells us that there is no condemnation for those who live in union with Christ.

You can't come to Jesus pretending. And you can't hide. He already knows who you are. He already knows the mistakes you made, the ones you will make, and even the mistakes you would make if you had the opportunity.

Throughout the Bible we read about characters who experience moments of intense shame. King David did some terrible things, but eventually he confessed those sins to God and found a way to move on in his calling. He refused to sit forever in his shame.

When the woman caught in adultery was dragged in front of Jesus, He first turned His attention to her accusers. After he had done away with them, He reminded her that He did not condemn her either. He told her, "Go and sin no more" (John 8:11 NKJV).

You can know those verses, though, and it's still hard to get their meaning into your heart and mind. That's why some of us need to read and repeat them again and again. Biblical truths are like stakes in the ground that keep your tent from blowing away in a storm.

God says the mistake doesn't matter. You're forgiven. What matters is how you handle the mistake.

Stacy

When you pause, look at the shame, and reflect upon yourself, you can grow. If all things work together for the good, we can use our shame as a teaching moment and opportunity for growth. I have a client who is a leader in the religious community, and he once said to me, "God doesn't make mistakes, but I do." I thought that was a good philosophy to live by—that it is okay to make mistakes as long as you are trying your best to do what's right. In fact, mistakes are the evidence of trying.

Reasonable expectations are key, but that can be difficult, especially if a person grew up under harsh or unreasonable standards. We all need to step back and take the time to ask ourselves, *Am I creating standards and expectations that fit my lifestyle, my schedule, my finances, and the people who are in my life?*

But even in self-help, we must stay mindful of grace and realistic expectations. Trust me, just because I'm a therapist doesn't mean my life is always smooth and trouble free. I mess up all the time. Sometimes even when I know better. But that's okay; we all do these things.

Anthony

I have a T-shirt that says, "Faith over Fear." Maybe I should get another one that says, "Grace over Guilt." I reached out to Stacy because I gave myself the grace to realize that I was a mess. I *am* a mess. Like, right now. Still.

But I was tired of sitting in that mess, stuck and anxious. I refused to let confusion and shame continue to shut me down. My life might still be messy sometimes, but I'm working and I'm trying, and I am determined to do better, day by day.

I will not let shame control me. This book is not the result of living a perfect life. It's coming out of hardship and struggle, sleepless nights, and long days when I felt like I could not catch my next breath. That's why we're writing this way. I wanted it to be like a conversation, not overly rehearsed. Some books feel too polished and perfect, more of a lecture than a conversation. That's not real to me.

Stacy

I feel the same way. People often think that we therapists have it all together and we expect our clients to have it all together. Neither of those things is true. I always say, "Focus on *progress over perfection*." Let's put that on a T-shirt too!

In our journeys for self-compassion, I find that we give grace to others a lot more quickly than we are willing to offer it to ourselves. Compassion for yourself is more difficult. But please offer yourself enough empathy to seek help.

There's no shame in therapy. It doesn't mean you're faithless or incapable of handling life. It just means you are invested in your emotional health and want to be the very best person you possibly can and that you need extra help to make that happen.

If you truly want to serve and help others, the best thing you can do is take care of yourself. Sometimes that means avoiding people who constantly point out your negative qualities and remind you of just how incapable you are. I don't know why that's so difficult for some of us, but it is. And being around those people can create shame inside us, even if they are actually the ones doing something shameful.

I want to say here and now to anyone who is involved in an abusive or neglectful relationship: it is not your fault. Set yourself free. Don't feel that you deserve it somehow or that you brought it upon yourself.

Anthony

We all know the story of Adam and Eve. They sinned and felt terrible shame. But God told them that He already knew; there was no need to hide. Even though their new reality was going to be different, God didn't call them out so He could punish them. Instead, it was to help them, in spite of their actions, to find a way to move forward.

Stacy

Even if you don't love or accept yourself in the moment, remember that God never stops loving you. We should all use Him as a role model and decide to never stop loving ourselves.

——————— STACY'S TIPS TO HELP YOU GET STARTED

- **REFLECTION:** Think about times you have felt shame. Was it due to your own view or the view of others? Look at your past. Have you been affected by people who shamed you or made you feel worthless or less than?
- **REALIZATION:** Take note of the people, places, and experiences that have led you to feel shame and assess how you might avoid or heal those experiences.
- **ACTION:** When you feel a sense of shame, investigate how that happened and why.

  - If you have done something you truly feel ashamed of, commit to never doing that again and move on from the shame.
  - If shame has you feeling stuck, force yourself to get moving. Get up, get out, exercise, go to church, give to others . . . do whatever it takes to lift the shame.

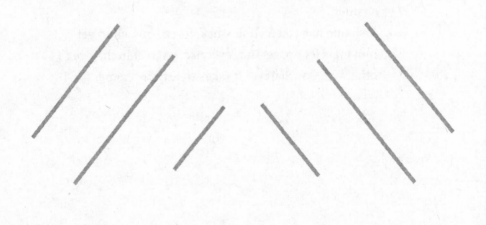

MISTAKES ARE THE EVIDENCE OF TRYING.

EIGHT

FEEL YOUR PAIN TO HEAL IT

*Sometimes it takes a painful experience to make us
change our ways.*

PROVERBS 20:30 GNT

Anthony

My drummer's name is Chris, but we call him Bebo. He's been with me
a long time and is like a little brother to me. Bebo's family is big into dirt
bikes and motocross, so his childhood memories are one huge blur of mud
and gasoline. I joked the other day that I was going to Bath & Body Works
to see if I could find Bebo a Texas dirt-and-gasoline candle so when we are
out on tour for a long stretch, he could light it and feel at home.

Bebo wrecked during a race one time, but everybody was watching
him, and dirt-bike riders have gotta be tough. So he got up limping and
tried to shake it off. Thing is, he couldn't shake it off. He was hurt badly.
Bebo has a lot of grit, so even though he couldn't finish the ride, he got
up and "walked it off."

Back in our junior high days there was this walk we all did to try to look cool. We'd have our Cross Colours overalls on with one strap undone, Fresh Prince–style high-top fade haircut, all while doing this side-to-side almost-limp down the hall to math class. Since everybody was walking like that anyway, Bebo figured out how to make his injury look like swag so nobody would know he was in pain. Pretty sharp—except one day Bebo's mom caught him walking that way.

"Boy, straighten up!" she ordered. "And stop trying to act cool! That's not who we are in this house."

Uh-oh. Bebo was busted. He couldn't straighten up and walk right. His mother took him to the doctor only to find out that all this time his hip had been out of place. Bebo had to have surgery to fix the pain that was being perceived as swag. To this day, Bebo has a screw in his hip. I bet if you asked, he would say he wishes he'd have sacrificed the cool and not been hurting for so long.

I believe a lot of us try to do something like this. Instead of admitting and addressing our emotional pain, we try to make it look like swag. Problem is, faking it gets old, and covering up can make a bad injury that much worse. Eventually you're busted—because if your mom doesn't call you out on it, God will.

Stacy

Pushing our pain away prevents us from healing, and it can eventually lead us to emotionally or physically harm ourselves or others because we haven't dealt with healing that pain. Maybe you've heard a saying that's popular in many recovery communities now: "Hurt people hurt people." In other words, abusive behavior often stems from unprocessed pain. If you or someone you are close to have been hurt, that hurt might get directed toward someone else.

We all carry baggage through life. Some of us have a carry-on small enough to fit under the seat. Others are pulling a luggage cart full of suitcases so filled to the brim that our undergarments are spilling out.

Baggage builds up from painful experiences, and those feelings continue to shape who we are, how we think, and the choices we make. What happens if you are carrying too much baggage? If you stuff it all down and try to shut the lid? It will weigh you down to the point that you can no longer move freely.

In therapeutic situations we often tell our clients, "You have to feel it to heal it." It's important that we give ourselves a chance not only to acknowledge our pain but to let ourselves have a moment to feel it.

Anthony

Stacy has what I call drop-the-mic moments. Sometimes I will walk into a session and five minutes in, she will hit me with *the truth*, like taking a scalpel and cutting straight into the wound to drain the poison out.

Welp, that's exactly what I needed to hear, I'll think. *I'm ready to go.* But since I signed up for the whole hour, we keep talking. Even while doing this book, I'm getting blessed with insight that helps. *Feel it to heal it.* That's good.

Stacy

Feeling it to heal it is not always easy. One of the best ways to heal pain is to share it with a safe person. I believe in telling your story to as many supportive people as possible. It looks and sounds different once you get it out of your head. The release will make you feel better, and many will want to reach out and help. There's no glory in suffering in silence alone.

Secrets can keep us sick, and tragedy can break anyone. No matter how capable or tough you are, eventually, something is going to come along and push you beyond your ability to cope.

Look, nobody likes being in pain, even though we all get our share of it. But if we try to stuff our pain down, it only shows up somewhere else. Pain can be hard to figure out, and just like a cut or a contusion, you might need a specialist's help. When the damage is too severe for a Band-Aid and some ibuprofen, that's where therapy might come in.

Anthony

Pain is like that Whac-a-Mole game at Chuck E. Cheese. Every time you try to push it down it's only going to pop up somewhere else.

Stacy

Exactly. If you don't take the time to look at your pain, it will pop back up when you least expect it. It might come out directed at you. It might come out directed at someone else.

For example, in therapy, a lot of clients will ask me, "Why am I in such a bad mood all the time? I don't want to be mean and nasty to people, but I am."

I'll usually pause before asking another question back. "Has something hurt you or upset you recently that you didn't really take the time to deal with?" Nine times out of ten, my client will nod slowly and say something like, "Yeah, I guess so. I really didn't think about it that way."

Anthony

Stacy has done that with me more than once. She used to tell me that pain was an indication that I needed to take a closer look at what was going on inside. I am supersensitive and I take on the feelings of the world around me, whether I like it or not. Somewhere along the way that would make me confused because my feelings would be so overwhelming that they would block me from being grateful, like I thought God wanted me to be. I'm just not a person who can go straight to quoting Scripture. First, I have to process what's going on inside.

Again, the Bible says it's okay to be angry, as long as we don't use it as an opportunity to sin or turn our hearts away from God (Ephesians 4:26). But I've learned there is freedom in the simple act of expressing pain without making excuses or apologizing or having to explain. That was a huge step for me.

I don't have to get everything resolved before I come to God. Jesus is still with me. Now I let the pain come and know that it's trying to send me an important message.

Stacy

Pain is your body and mind's way of telling you that you are hurting, much like the check-engine light on your car.

Anthony

One time I was super busy and ended up driving, like, three whole weeks with my check-engine light on. I didn't have time to deal with it. Guess what happened?

I ended up with a bigger problem.

A $200 repair ended up costing $1,500. Ignore it long enough and you can ruin your car.

Our objective in this chapter is to encourage everyone reading not only to acknowledge your emotional "check-engine light" but to find out why it's on. That will be the beginning of a smoother ride through life.

Proverbs 21:5 tells us that hard work and good planning lead to prosperity, but if you rush and try to take shortcuts, it's only going to lead to poverty. Pushing feelings aside and pretending like everything is okay might keep you moving for now, but it'll catch up with you at some point. That shortcut you thought you were taking only leads to a dead end.

None of this pain stuff is new. And for sure, it affects everyone. If you've lived any time at all, you have struggled with trying to figure the way out of emotional, physical, and spiritual pain. In fact, I bet many of you are wrestling with some form of severe pain right now.

Stacy

Emotional pain activates the same areas of your brain as physical pain. That means heartache hits you just the same as if we had put your hand on a hot stove. Keep that in mind when you feel like the pain is hard to control.

Anthony

What's wild about that is it means emotional pain really *is* physical pain. It affects your brain. But you can't see it like a cut or a gunshot wound. The damage is on the inside.

Whether an engine or an arm, when anything in your life breaks, it would be ridiculous not to go see a professional for help. But if it's a broken heart or severe disappointment? *Suck it up! Why can't you just get over it?*

Stacy

That's right! No matter if it's physical, emotional, or spiritual—pain is pain and it hurts. You might be able to ignore it for a while, but pain has a way of becoming so loud and merciless that it drowns out every other good thing in life.

Anthony

After recognizing suffering and pain, our desire should be not to mask it but to deal with it. If suffering is like a gas, masking will ultimately mean that the pressure becomes too much.

I believe the pain that results from trauma can be turned into triumph. (Oh man, that sounded just like something my dad would say! Which is probably why it just popped into my head.)

I know that's true because I've lived it, but also because I have seen others walk through their own painful circumstances and come out stronger on the other side.

There's a model in Los Angeles named Winnie Harlow. She has a condition called vitiligo, which leaves patches of skin without pigment. She grew up being traumatized and ostracized because she looks different. I don't know Winnie personally, but what I do know is that she took a very traumatic situation and turned it into a victory. She is now considered a supermodel. You see, her rare condition, when coupled with hard work and confidence, has become the reason she's featured on runways and campaigns all over the world. Her ability to overcome is an example to others, and she has turned what most would consider a setback into a platform to let others who are different know that there is a place in the world for them too.

But when we are in the middle of a trial, the possibility that the thing causing us the most pain might become the thing that creates the most progress makes zero sense.

Stacy

Not until we look back and realize, *Now I know why this happened. It was terrible and hard, but it really did work out for the good.*

Anthony

There are ministries that have not yet been born, books and songs that will not be written until we have walked through the fire and come out on the other side. God's grace is sufficient, but that doesn't mean I don't still struggle in the trials. When it hurts, I don't want the lessons that come from overcoming or suffering. I just want the pain to stop.

I'm not only writing this for others; it's for me too. In the meantime, the best we can do is reach out to someone who is going through something similar. Be a support. When we help others, it helps us too.

Stacy

Moving beyond pain requires kindness and compassion for others and for yourself. I have clients who will describe some awful ordeal to me, and I will reply with, "That sounds like it was very traumatic for you."

"Well, I don't know. Not really," they'll say. "I've got friends who have been through so much worse."

If I break my arm and meet someone with two broken arms, I might feel a moment of gratitude, sure, and I can be thankful that it wasn't worse. But I still walk away with a broken arm. Suffering isn't a competition. There is no comfort in comparison.

When people are hurt, they often just want to hide out until the pain lets up. That's the worst thing you can do. If you are emotionally low, you need to move. Physical movement releases emotional pain. Go for a walk. Trim your hedges. Knead bread. Make pizza dough. Anthony has his "Yes I Will" remix that's good for dancing. Moving is a helpful way to deal with sadness, frustration, and emotional pain.

Anthony

That's why, for me, exercise is so important. I can be having the worst day ever, but if I get my heart rate up and sweat, do some planks, put the gloves on and punch that heavy bag at my favorite gym—I will always feel better than when I walked in. Every time.

Stacy

Exercise is a legitimate way to boost endorphins and release pain. Crying is good too. There's no shame in letting out tears. Research has shown that it releases toxins from your body and relieves stress.[4]

Sometimes I will tell people to have a good cry, and they'll say to me, "Oh no. I can't do that. I am not the kind of person who cries."

"Okay," I'll suggest. "Then put on a movie or a song that speaks to whatever you are going through right now. Something you can really relate to. Then give yourself permission to feel whatever feelings come. If it's tears, fine. Or anger, crushing sadness, regret. Whatever is honest, let it rise to the surface."

There are no wrong emotions. It's only problematic when we try to suppress our true feelings. It doesn't matter *how* you release it, just that you let it out.

Anthony

Crying is hard for a lot of people because it feels weak, like you can't hold it together. The Bible says that, apart from God, none of us can hold it together (John 15:5). That's why Jesus came to help. It also says that when we are weak, He is strong (2 Corinthians 12:9–11), and that if we humble ourselves before the Lord, He will lift us up (James 4:10).

I'll admit my emotions first. I'm a big guy from Dallas, Texas, who rides horses, loves to spar in the boxing ring—and sometimes I cry. I remember in one session with Stacy, I was bawling so hard that I couldn't even see straight. It felt like everything in my life was falling apart and I could not even get the words out. It was an incredibly humbling experience.

No, scratch that. It was humiliating. Here I was, a grown man, collapsing into a mess of snot and tears, not able to speak. Even if that person sitting across from you is a thoughtful and professional therapist, it's still embarrassing to sit there while they watch you weep.

Down where I grew up, if you started to cry, a lot of adults would glare at you and say, "Boy, you'd better stop that crying before I give you something to cry about."

So you learn to hold it all inside. But I got to a point where I had to let it go instead.

Stacy

Therapists see crying as a positive sign. It's a step toward releasing pain and healing. But in some situations, with some people, it is not safe to cry.

97

Losing control of our emotions is still hard, even in front of a counselor. We understand that and make sure to remind our clients that they are in a nonjudgmental environment. The therapist's office should be the safest place in the world to reveal your messiest and most authentic self.

Anthony

When Stacy let me know that crying was part of healing, that was monumental for me. It was difficult in the moment, but I walked out of her office feeling so much lighter and freer. I can testify to that verse in James 4:10—I had to humble myself, and it was totally uncomfortable. But once I did, God lifted me up.

Stacy

Sometimes, dwelling on feelings for too long can be hard as well. People will often come to me stuck and unable to get over something from their past, whether the traumatic event happened five years ago or twenty-five years ago.

So, yes, it is important to feel that pain and process it. But we cannot allow ourselves to get stuck in that pain. There is a time to play sad songs and have a good cry. One important point that is often overlooked: *don't forget to breathe.*

When someone is in physical pain, like childbirth, the medical staff will remind you to breathe. That's why an ob-gyn will suggest breathing classes to prepare for labor. Even when you get a massage, and they are digging in deep to get the knots out, the massage therapist will say, "Deep breath. Breathe. Let it all out."

Breathing is a fundamental way to relieve emotional pain as well. Here's a simple exercise you can do right now: breathe in deeply for the count of four seconds and exhale out for eight. It helps relieve stress in your body, which will reduce some of the pain.

Anthony

There have been moments when I've been able to better engage in my faith because I have sat in a quiet place and simply breathed deep, focused, and chilled. If your mind is racing, you've got to find a way to get still.

Stacy

Pain isn't pleasant, but it can change us for the good. It can make a person stronger, humbler, more compassionate. Pain can help clarify what's important in life. And as we learn all we can do to cope with pain in a healthy way—to process and breathe through it—we can also look for the lesson in the pain. It can be a great teacher.

————— STACY'S TIPS TO HELP YOU GET STARTED

- **REFLECTION:** The first step to dealing with pain is to acknowledge it by reflecting on the source and why you are hurting. We titled this chapter "Feel Your Pain to Heal It" for a reason. The truth is, you *are* already feeling it; you just need to allow yourself a moment to let it be known, and then say something to yourself like, "I am really hurting over this (insert the source of the pain)." Pain can happen when you lose someone or something. It could be a job, a person—anything. Pain can be inflicted by someone else; someone could have hurt your feelings or physically hurt you. You can become emotionally pained by something you saw on social media. It's important to notice when you have been hit with some level of pain.
- **REALIZATION:** It is important to realize that pain makes some people uncomfortable, and sometimes sharing pain makes the person listening feel something unpleasant too. As a result of whatever is

going on for that person, they might try to fix your pain by offering you some ice cream or an alcoholic beverage. Some people will suggest that something shouldn't be bothering you. "Just let it go," they will say. Easier said than done. I think most of you would agree that you would happily let go of your pain if it were that easy to do. Realize that sharing your pain can be a messy business, and know that you always have the option to see a professional counselor and the right to process your pain in a way that's healthy for you.

- **ACTION:** After the important work of acknowledging that you do have pain, take these essential steps:

  - Make sure you are taking care of your basic needs: food, water, and sleep. Many of us neglect those things while we are suffering.
  - Be patient and compassionate with yourself; healing takes time.
  - Share the story of your pain with a safe and trusted friend, family member, or counselor. As I mentioned, telling your story is healing.
  - Remember that bad experiences, trauma, and pain do not define you.

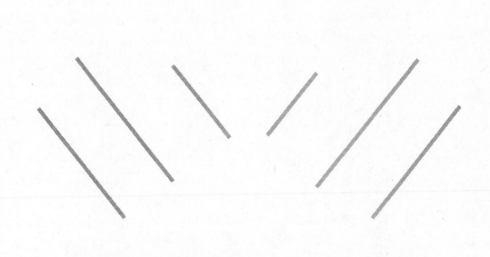

PROGRESS CAN ONLY START WITH TRUTH.

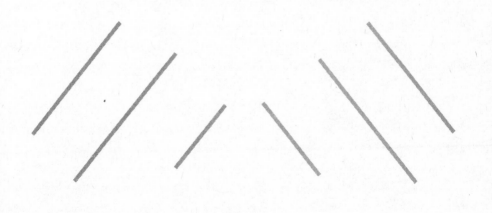

$$\boxed{\text{NINE}}$$

RECOGNIZE YOUR
TOXIC PEOPLE

*Be sober [well balanced and self-disciplined], be
alert and cautious at all times. That enemy of yours,
the devil, prowls around like a roaring lion [fiercely
hungry], seeking someone to devour.*

1 PETER 5:8 AMP

Anthony

I love animals, and I can't get enough of watching the Discovery
Channel and Animal Planet. Some days I keep it on in the background
just because I have a little ADD (*squirrel!*) and sometimes I need extra
cognitive stimulation. Maybe you also have favorite "background
noise" TV shows you choose to help you not feel bored or buried in a
project.

One afternoon I looked up from my computer to watch a show about predatory animals. I'd seen it a hundred times but could not keep from watching again.

It was the stereotypical precious, panting, and parched gazelle who simply wanted a drink of water. The beautiful animal's options were few, so she cautiously crept to the edge of the brown pond that looked toxic and dangerous. She was thirsty, though, and her options were limited. So she moved in for a drink.

"Don't do it!" I shouted at the screen.

After frantically looking in every direction, the frail creature took a few more hesitant steps to the water's edge. Putting her head down, she took a quick sip before pulling up with fear in her eyes.

The gazelle glanced around before going for another drink, this time a bit longer. Then another sip with more confidence because she had started to feel safe.

We all know how this story ends. A ten-foot crocodile was unbelievably camouflaged just an inch under the surface. He lunged forth to seize her neck. She fought but had no chance of surviving because the crocodile not only had a grip but had pulled her into his environment, the water, where he maneuvered freely.

You may be reading this story thinking, *Anthony has lost it. Why in the world are we talking about* Animal Planet, *gazelles, and crocodiles right now?*

Some of us are so thirsty for relationship that we ignore the warning signs until it is too late. Subsequently we are trapped because of our compromise. We lose sight of the danger because of what we so desperately needed and fall prey to a thirst trap.

Toxic relationships are one of the main things that led me to Stacy's couch. Most everyone struggles with balance, boundaries, and knowing when to walk away in relationships. For people of faith, the subject can be especially difficult because we've been taught to forgive and turn the other cheek. Too many times, "forgiveness" puts us right back in that dangerous pond.

Stacy

Clients and friends ask me all the time, "Is my relationship toxic? What does a toxic relationship look like?"

From a therapist's point of view, if you have to ask that question, you might very well be in a toxic relationship. Typically, if the relationship is going great, you don't spend a lot of time questioning whether it is healthy.

Anthony

Stacy helped me realize that I have codependent tendencies that open me up to toxic relationships. Sometimes I take on too much responsibility for what people around me are doing, and I get so worried about how and what they are doing that I stop trusting myself, my own feelings, or my own needs. Most often I don't even realize I have other options. But I can't always blame the other person because I am the one opening the door to let them in.

Or, if I liken it to the story of the gazelle, I'm the one who keeps creeping down to the water's edge. I had to turn my focus to working on my own issues and making my vision clearer.

Stacy has taught me that self-awareness is an important key to healthy relationships. Being in tune with my emotions helps me build up a radar for dysfunction and makes me more aware of what is healthy and what is not. It's kind of like when you clean up your diet and start exercising. Your tastes change. Those fries might still be tempting, but you know they're not good for you, so it's easier to stay away because they would counter all the work you've done. You don't have to eat a jumbo bag of waffle fries and then feel regret. Self-awareness helps you put the brakes on before things go too far.

Stacy

I *love* waffle fries.

Anthony

Me too. I used to work out for an hour and then order a couple of super sizes and tear through them all at once. Then, of course, I would get sick and be miserable. There's shame again. Waffle fries are okay in appropriate doses and . . . anyway, there goes the short attention span again.

Not every relationship is going to be perfectly open and healthy because we're all broken in different places. Every relationship is a little dysfunctional. But when you get in tune with your emotions, you can tell when something is not good for you and stop before it gets out of hand. You can make a quality decision on the front end instead of managing a crisis because you got into a bad situation.

With toxic people, you have to keep your antenna up. The Bible verse from Peter at the beginning of this chapter tells us to be clear-minded, alert, and cautious, because the Enemy is prowling and seeking someone to devour. I'm not saying a toxic person in your life is evil or possessed, but if we are not careful, we will connect to others in our sickness rather than in healthy ways. And the enemies that devour us are anxiety, fear, depression, and shame.

Stacy

Many of us know what it is like to be caught up in a dysfunctional relationship. You are never sure where you stand, and the emotions are far too intense. Relationships marked by extremes—by fear and clinging, soaring highs and crashing lows, substance abuse, lies, instability, walking on eggshells, a general baseline of chaos—are far more toxic than gorging on waffle fries. As a matter of fact, in my twenty-five years as a therapist, *no one* has ever come to me crying that their waffle fries inflicted pain on them!

In case you were wondering, those of us who counsel others can also fall victim to toxic people. Some of them are family members. (Can I get a witness?) But also, many toxic people come disguised as good humans, so it is easy to get lured in. Like Anthony said, the crocodile lies camouflaged right beneath the surface.

We therapists can easily fall victim to believing we can rescue or fix others. That is why so many kindhearted helpers see what we believe to be the good in people and overlook all the red flags, hoping that our support will change their toxicity. Truth is, people only change as they truly desire change, and toxic people rarely believe they need to change.

Anthony

It's rare that anyone who works in entertainment wears business suits in Los Angeles. You show up to a meeting looking trendy, and your car is more like your business suit. But if you go into a Ferrari dealership, it doesn't matter how sharply dressed or fancy you might look—they are going to run a credit check to make sure you're who you appear to be.

Maybe we need to run emotional credit checks on people before we give them full access to our lives.

The Bible has a lot to say about how appearances can be deceiving. John 7:24 tells us to stop judging by appearances and instead look at standards that are true. In Ephesians, we are told, "Let no one deceive you with empty words" (5:6). And Matthew talks about those who look great on the outside but on the inside are filled with deception and hypocrisy (23:27).

Smiles can be deceiving. Charm can be deceiving. Personality can be deceiving. Take the time to run a credit history on the people in your life. Observe how they treat, talk about, and care for others. It will help you determine if they can afford the investment of a relationship with you.

Stacy

The credit check at the car dealer takes only a few minutes, but with people and relationships it should take a lot more time and be an ongoing process. People need to earn our trust. After earning it, they need to work to maintain it—much like continuing to pay your bills on time so you can maintain good financial credit.

The saying has been around so long you'd think we'd have learned by now: you can't judge a book by its cover.

Anthony

Except for the Bible.

Stacy

Or this book, hopefully.

Anthony

Sticking with the Ferrari analogy, I read a story awhile back about a man who won a new Ferrari Portofino. Even though he got the car for free, he couldn't afford the upkeep. Required maintenance is something like three thousand dollars a year, and that doesn't include tires! Even though the car was beautiful and the man loved it, he had to sell his Ferrari.

The Bible also says that before you take something on, use wisdom and count the cost (Luke 14:28). I'm not suggesting that we become high maintenance, but relationships require work and sacrifice. And it's a two-way street. You should know that you are worth the investment and prove that belief through your actions.

Stacy

If you are not reading between the lines of what we have already said, let me say it clearly: Toxic relationships typically start out great. They look wonderful. They're interesting and fun. I often hear someone saying, "He or she was *so* amazing when we first met."

Then, four or five months later, the walls start to cave in.

People can't be phony for long. Pretending and covering your tracks is too much work. Eventually cracks begin to show. Maybe for a few weeks you hold that anger in, but sooner or later you lose it and scream at a loved one or curse out the cashier at Starbucks for getting your order wrong. You can hide your drinking for a few weeks, but eventually you show up smelling like alcohol and slurring your words. Whatever the relationship, it's important to allow enough time for someone to show consistency.

Something else a lot of people tell me is, "I'm in a poisonous relationship, but my friends and family think they are wonderful." That's because others are only seeing the external facade and not what goes on in secret, behind closed doors.

The opposite can happen as well, when the people in your life see a friend or partner is not treating you the way they should. This is sometimes what we observe when people are victims of abuse and cannot see the toxicity for themselves. In these situations, a support system made up of people who know and care is critical in helping to highlight what needs to change.

I call this phenomenon "relationship by committee." If your trusted friends, family, and therapist, aka the committee, are all telling you that you need to open your eyes, you need to take a good hard look at the relationship you are in.

Anthony

It usually takes a little time living in a situation before you can truly tell what's going on. I recently bought a new house, and it's nice, and I am very thankful for God's blessing. It looks so beautiful from the street. But after I had lived there a few months, I realized there were a lot of problems going on beneath the surface—problems that were the builder's responsibility to fix. The longer I tried to ignore the problems, the bigger they became and the more I had to push on the builder to address them.

Some of the issues were common or the kind of regular maintenance that you wouldn't know about if you had been living in an apartment. But there were also structural issues that came from a defect in the construction. Once I discovered those problems, I had a decision to make. How much was I willing to invest in this, and how much time could I spend waiting on this builder to get it together? Should I even switch builders? Could I turn this house into a refuge and safe place to live? Because if I did not choose wisely, the damage and lack of fulfilled promises of "I'll get it handled" could pull me under.

If a person has serious foundational issues that go back to childhood and they have been living in decades of dysfunction, you are not likely to "fix" them with your love and devotion. Songs and movies would like for us to believe that, but it usually isn't realistic.

Stacy

Can I say it in a more direct way? We should not be spending time with people who bring us down. It doesn't matter who you are or where you go; there are broken, hurt, toxic people everywhere.

Yes, God wants us to help others. We believe in forgiveness and grace. We understand the importance of patience and that it is wrong to judge. All that said, it is not healthy to continue to engage in a relationship where you are suffering. Keep in mind, there is no such thing as perfection in relationships, friendships, families, or careers. But we also need to make sure that we are caring for ourselves—especially when we are dealing with those who are not caring for us.

Anthony

There's this verse I know, but at some level I wasn't acting like it. Maybe you've heard it: "Do not be misled: 'Bad company corrupts good character'" (1 Corinthians 15:33). I was staying in dysfunctional relationships because I thought I was good and strong enough to pull someone else up. I thought I could rescue them. But something else was happening. Their need for me made me feel valuable, so I returned again and again and again.

There is nothing wrong with being there for a person whose head is under life's water. But as I learned in lifeguard certification back when I was sixteen, if someone is drowning, you swim toward them, stop about four feet away, and then proceed to give them the tools they need to float. You never swim right up to a panicked, flailing swimmer, because in their instinctive need to survive they will pull you under. It's not because they are innately bad, but because they want to keep their head above water so they can live.

Our value should come from God—not our ability to fix, change, or save someone. That path will most likely lead to us drowning.

Stacy

The irony in trying to help a toxic person see their value or build them up is that these dysfunctional people, like Anthony mentioned, will often break us down while we are trying to lift them up.

Anthony

It's like running a marathon in bad shoes. Running a marathon is tough. You've got 26.2 miles of pounding your feet on pavement, sometimes in blazing heat or freezing temps, running uphill or down. It's hard enough to make that trek in the best of conditions. Can you imagine trying to do it in shoes that don't fit? I even know a few hardcore runners who have shoes specially crafted to fit their arches and running style.

What if I tried to run the Los Angeles Marathon in a pair of shoes two sizes too small that I got because they were on sale? Maybe I loved the design and thought others would be impressed. You know what would happen if I tried to run twenty-six miles in too-tight shoes that were impressive to others but didn't fit me? I'd be in a wheelchair by mile eight.

Relationships, like marathons, are tough. I bet you know someone who gets themselves into one bad "doesn't fit" situation after another with friends or romance. And you're thinking, *Why are they hanging out with that person? Can't they see what the rest of us see?*

Have you ever looked at wedding pictures and just shaken your head because you knew the couple wasn't a good fit for each other? And when the road gets long and hard, you know there is going to be trouble.

Oh, and one other thing—often, when you're planning on running a marathon, an experienced salesperson will encourage you to go up a size because of the swelling that might happen due to the distance. This is the same principle in romantic relationships and even in friendships, and maybe why people say, "Marry up!"

You need people who can go the distance with you in all ways. And those people need you too. Proverbs 13:20 offers a warning about dysfunctional relationships: "Walk with the wise and become wise, for a companion of fools suffers harm."

Stacy

Let's talk about the signs of a dysfunctional relationship, because it can be very hard to see them while you are in one.

Sometimes you are dealing with overtly abusive, angry, or nasty people, but toxicity can also come from someone who is controlling in ways that are quieter, more passive-aggressive, and difficult to detect. Have you ever been in a relationship where you constantly thought, *Am I the irrational one here? Am I imagining things? Is it me?* Those of us who are growth oriented will stop and ask ourselves, *Is it me?* But if the inappropriate, frustrating, or abusive behaviors are coming from the other person, then the only thing that is on you might be why you would put up with those behaviors.

Anthony

Stacy put a post on Instagram that said, "From a distance, a fistful of red flags can look a lot like roses." It was brilliant, but it also shows why we need to work on focusing our emotional vision or having friends around who have non-emotional vision and can give us perspective. Because by the time you get too close, it might be too late to put the brakes on your emotions.

Stacy

God first speaks in a whisper. If that doesn't work, He throws a brick at your head.

Anthony

How many times have I been told that in a session? More than I can remember. I think it's so important to learn to listen and avoid God having to lovingly yet aggressively get my attention.

Stacy

I say that to people all the time. Learn to look for the small signs; don't wait until the red flags turn into fireworks. It is difficult for some of us to do this, but we need to see things for what they are rather than what we wish they were.

Quality relationships take work, but they shouldn't be marked by misery and difficulty. They are not supposed to inflict pain. That doesn't mean you won't experience painful moments; all relationships have those. But when the pain is inflicted by the other person, or you find you are suffering more than you are not, it's important to take a good hard look at the relationship and ask yourself some important questions.

Are you compromising all the time? Can you really be yourself? Is there always stress, always some drama? Do you struggle to hold on to joy and peace?

Anthony

Let's say it's late in the game. The yellow flags have turned red, and you are in deep. What are some practical ways to detach from a toxic person?

Stacy

Some of my clients are stuck in toxic relationships and will try to rationalize them by saying, "But God says I am supposed to stay with this person forever!" I hear that from a faith-based perspective often, and theologically it can be a very difficult situation to get a handle on. Gather plenty of support from therapists, mentors, ministers—everyone you can—before taking such a step.

Anthony

Not too long ago I dog-sat for one of my close friends. It was just a few days with an eighty-four-pound puppy that thought he belonged on my white couch. Anyway, after playing with him for a while, I decided to feed him.

The second I gave him the food, he scarfed it down. He finished before I could count to five. Almost as quickly after, he looked at me with a face that said, *I shouldn't have done that.* The knowing look on this dog's face made me panic and say aloud, "You better not throw up on my hide rug."

Before I could get the words out, every ounce of his dinner was on my rug! Grossed out and mad, I ran to get paper towels as fast as I could. I wasn't quick enough, though, because I turned back to find—you guessed it—the puppy giving his dinner another try right off the rug.

I couldn't handle it. I thought, *Who in the world would ever think that returning to your own vomit would be an option?* Then, as quick as I was able to get mad at him, I remembered Proverbs 26:11, "As a dog returns to its vomit, so fools repeat their folly."

Wow, I thought. *I should be just as grossed out and angry at the toxic relationships and scenarios I willfully take back in, just because they are there.*

Stacy

If the relationship is hurtful or disappointing, why would you take it back in? Most times, though, making that decision to walk away is easier said than done.

When defining a toxic relationship, consider a couple of points. Does your compassion leave you hurt? Are you always coming up short? This is why therapists encourage clients to find support in other places. For example, if your significant other doesn't build you up, you need to find other sources of fresh water. (And for the record, I don't mean an affair. I mean guidance to empower yourself to deal with a difficult situation.)

It's always important to stay busy and get involved in activities with people who will listen and lift you up. Sometimes a person has been so beaten down and brainwashed, they must build up strength to even begin taking appropriate action. Again, this book is not meant to be a substitute for seeking help from a professional. We just want to offer an on-ramp and help you see how faith and pursuing good mental health are not contradictions.

Another way to deal with a toxic attachment is to create as much distance as possible. Someone might say, "My sister is so mean and critical that it makes me dread family get-togethers. It takes me three days to get over the abuse of one afternoon."

Sometimes we all get trapped in the fire. Invite a friend in hopes that your sibling will be on better behavior. Plan to make your time with that person as short as possible so the pain is minimized. Volunteer to work in the kitchen so you limit your time in the room with that toxic person. Sometimes we have to get creative to take care of ourselves. But the over-arching message I would like you to know is that we must choose distance over disrespect!

Hey, another T-shirt we all need!

Anthony

Codependency will make you think, *If I get rid of this person, what will I have left?*

Stacy

Peace! It's better to have peace alone than turmoil in a crowd. But some people will do anything rather than be alone with themselves, even if it costs them their physical, emotional, or spiritual well-being. The first step out of that kind of situation is to become aware of what is toxic and what is not. We'll continue talking about ways of dealing with toxic people in the next chapter.

STACY'S TIPS TO HELP YOU GET STARTED

- **REFLECTION:** Take time to assess who in your life is toxic and any role you have played in enabling that person or continuing to invest in that person. Allowing toxic behaviors can send the toxic person the message that you are okay with what they are doing. It is important to note here that toxic people *love* those of us who have a high tolerance for their bad behaviors.
- **REALIZATION:** While we have spent time in this chapter discussing how to identify these toxic people, it is important to understand that they are everywhere. You will meet them no matter what; and if you are a kind, growth-oriented, and compassionate person, they may try to convince you to continue to engage with them in spite of how they treat you.
- **ACTION:** Once you have identified your toxic individuals, take these action steps.

make an impact. If I help them, they might grow. I'm not perfect either. Maybe I need to cut them some slack.

In comparison, people with less empathy don't have as much tolerance for inappropriate behaviors. They are much quicker to say goodbye and mean it.

Anthony

Stacy let me know that I was the kind of person who sees the best in people and forgets that it may be accompanied by the worst. I want to help but end up making excuses for the way they are treating me, because through the cracks and underneath the rubble, I see something valuable.

Stacy

Anyone who knows Anthony knows he is filled with empathy. It's a beautiful gift for those who have received it. But life grows difficult when you become dependent on a toxic person. You start to *need* them in your life, which makes you more willing to overlook the warning signs. This does nothing for your self-esteem and can ultimately impact your ability to be successful and happy in life.

Just today, a client said, "My mother keeps screaming at me, and I cannot figure out what I'm doing wrong."

"Have you done anything that you feel hasn't been good or right?" I asked.

"No," she replied. "I wait on her hand and foot. I came into the living room with her dinner, and she cursed and threw the TV remote at me."

"What happened then?" I asked.

"The remote smacked against the wall right next to my head. I just put her tray down and walked back out the door."

"What would've happened if you had said, 'Mom, I know you're upset right now, but it is not okay to throw things at me.'"

"Oh my gosh," she exclaimed. "I don't think I could ever say anything like that."

I paused to let the weight of her words sink in. Then I looked directly in her eyes and calmly told her, "It's not you. It's not your fault. We cannot control the behavior of others, only our own behavior."

As the message sank in, tears began to stream down my client's cheeks. "All this time, I've been blaming myself," she said sadly. "All these years, I have been thinking there must be something I'm not doing right."

That's a good example of how having the space and permission to say something out loud can help someone see their situation clearly for the first time. What message did my client send by walking out of the room? *Treat me however you want. I will never confront you or do anything about it.*

Anthony

When we take on the blame or are convinced that we must be doing something wrong, that to me equates to questioning our value. That's what happens when we allow ourselves to "go on sale."

I was in Beverly Hills the other day, just driving through, and I noticed that you never see a high-end car dealership—for instance, a Ferrari dealer—with a sale sign on their window. "No money down, easy financing, 0 percent APR!" They don't run those specials on exceptionally well-crafted automobiles. Why? Because those dealers aren't trying to attract people who can't afford the experience.

I'm not saying that from an egotistical point of view, like we should think of ourselves as luxury cars, but actually the Bible *does* say that we were created in God's image and that we are of great value to Him (Genesis 1:27; Luke 12:7). Also, that we are fearfully and wonderfully made (Psalm 139:14).

You will never see anything that is a one-of-a-kind on sale. Guess what? You are one of a kind! When we discount ourselves, it doesn't help us or the other person.

That's what I was doing. I was putting myself on sale with easy, low-cost terms. No big investment necessary. You don't have to put in the time, work, or care. I will work enough for both of us. But the truth is that relationships require investment, maintenance, and accountability from both people.

I had to cut some people out of my life. It hurt and it was hard, and at times it was heartbreaking. But we were not good for each other. Those spaces have been filled with healthier relationships where the river of blessing flows both ways. We encourage each other and help each other grow. We both put in the necessary work. That would never have happened without my setting boundaries and refusing to return to my foolishness.

Most of us have found ourselves trapped in a toxic situation. Maybe it's a spouse or a child or a parent. What can you do if you don't feel like there's an escape?

Stacy

If you can't limit physical space, then limit mental space. Refuse to participate in the chaos. Do not let them draw you in. If you don't feel strong enough to stand up, then work on building up those muscles until you can. It may take time.

I was speaking with someone yesterday who said to me, "I keep getting blindsided by my father."

"Stop getting blindsided. He's your father. You've known him your whole life and he's always been this way," I replied. "You need to start expecting it. Expect that the minute you speak to him, he is going to launch into the list of reasons why you're not a good enough daughter. Don't go on that phone call believing everything is going to be wonderful this time. Go in fully prepared for the fact that he is going to complain that you don't call him enough, that you're a terrible daughter, that you should be more appreciative, call more often, spend more time. Brace yourself for the blow so you can absorb it better. Do not let him draw you in."

Anthony

If you refuse to engage, often that person will get mad and ramp up the taunts. It's hard to be a spectator when they are trying to lure you into the game. I would constantly have to reset my mind and attitude. Sometimes you have to mentally buckle yourself into life's seat as a spectator and take full control of your emotional engagement.

Stacy

You may have heard of a practice in some therapy circles called the gray rock method. If you are dealing with a difficult person, you become like a "gray rock." Unemotional. Brief. Boring. In other words, you refuse to play their game.

Being a person of faith does not mean that you must put up with mistreatment. You are not stuck with people who don't lift you up or make you feel valued. Limit their access and ability to make you feel ugly, worthless, stupid, or less than enough.

Anthony

Recently I went on a vacation with a friend. Wires got crossed and things between us became heated and tense. I immediately began to look up return flights and was ready to book a flight for home when I remembered what Stacy had suggested about assessing the value of the relationship. Although I had my flight on hold, I decided to stay and try talking about the issue at hand before I made a rash decision to simply leave. In this case, apologies were exchanged and the trip and the friendship ended up being better than before.

In the moment, I had to ask myself if it was worth it—if I had the resolve to deal with it and if I wanted to stop making assumptions and creating my own narrative just so I could avoid conflict.

It is much harder to make the commitment to communicate, listen, and work on resolving conflict. You always take a risk with confrontation of any kind. That person could double down or refuse to budge. Either way, though, it's better to know where you stand.

The old Anthony would have stormed off hurt and angry. It would have been a terrible, angsty plane ride home, and once I got home, I would've stewed over the situation for a long time. But the new Anthony knows that doesn't have to happen.

Stacy

Every quality relationship has challenges. It's important to remember that difficulty does not always mean toxicity.

Anthony

We were in a session once, and Stacy said to me, "Ultimately, what you permit, you teach." That one line changed everything. In that moment, the lights came on. It's not selfish to take care of yourself and to avoid instructing people that treat you badly. Your passivity could become part of the reason a relationship becomes toxic.

Stacy

I said it because I see it happening all the time. We need to think about the messages we are sending people. Standing up for yourself is good for self-esteem, even if you can't change the person who is treating you badly. And when you let them treat you poorly, you reinforce that it is okay to treat others that way as well.

We must teach people how to treat us. Really, it's one of the most loving things we can do. Plus, our faith encourages kindness—even to ourselves.

Anthony

As I mentioned earlier, if I offer someone front-row seats in my life because I fear those seats will be empty, even if that person is disruptive or disrespectful, it communicates that I'm okay having someone around who treats me poorly. I'm saying it's better to give them a place than risk having no one at all.

News flash! That thinking is *not* trusting God or having faith that He can help us move better friends into our lives.

Stacy

I posted this on my Instagram story recently: "It's important to know that sometimes considerate and overly kind people are that way because they were raised in fear of upsetting someone."

If you are one of those people who doesn't speak up because you're afraid of upsetting yourself or others, you need to practice so you can build up your voice. Even if it's just in the grocery store. If someone cuts in line, you can say, "Excuse me, you just got in front of me." Or if a family member criticizes you, you might say, "That hurt my feelings," or "Let's try to speak to each other with kindness." You don't have to be aggressive or confrontational. Just find a space to start speaking up for yourself. The more you practice, the better you will get at it, and the more those around you will learn that you do not tolerate being treated badly.

Anthony

Have y'all seen *Sister Act 2*? That's a classic for me. There's a moment where Sister Mary Clarence is leading the school choir performance, and she calls a kid up to solo on "Oh Happy Day." His voice is weak and cracking, his eyes on the floor. The people in attendance exchange unimpressed looks. Sister Mary stirs him up, makes him sing a few scales, and through the magic of movie inspiration, two minutes later he's killing it and the crowd is on their feet.

What changed? He found what was already there. He learned how to use his voice. In real life it might not happen as fast as it did for him, but it can and will happen if you just keep singing.

Sometimes people don't want us to find strength or use our voices. They would rather keep us quiet with eyes down. I don't believe that's the life God has called us to live. We have to step up and use our voices. When we do, our feelings will follow our feet. If you act strong, you will feel strong.

Stacy

These are great points. But what happens when you do your best to voice your feelings in a calm and respectful manner, and that person dismisses you or tries to turn it around?

Anthony

They are showing me who they are. That makes it much easier to move on. People who refuse to respect our feelings should lose their seat at the table. A friend of mine says, "If you just watch and listen, people will show you who they are." The hard part is truly listening and being willing to face the truth and believe them, even if the truth is not what you want it to be.

Most of those people I thought were so important, but didn't respect me, are out of my life now. It's not that I don't love them, not that I didn't want the best for them. I had to choose wisdom, maturity, moving on, and keeping my head above water. It took letting go of the past to hold on to and move into the future God wanted for me. And last but not least, letting go of them says loudly and clearly, "I trust God with you."

It's important to add that these changes did not happen overnight. I still struggle with wanting to return to these toxic relationships sometimes, even to this day.

Stacy

This is a good place to talk about takeaways. What are some ways to deal with a person who doesn't respect your boundaries? Are these normal relationship hitches, or is it toxic?

Some people will not move so willingly from the front row to the balcony. Other times, to stay with the analogy, the toxic person is one of our costars on stage. We cannot move that person, and neither can we move away. In these cases, one of the first things we should do is seek to understand their qualities. Identifying their triggers will help us manage a difficult relationship.

Minimizing contact is crucial, but if you are forced to continue with this person, you want to set clear boundaries. Bring other people around to serve as a buffer, as toxic people are more prone to attack and lash out when one-on-one. Maybe you've heard the saying, "People come into your life for a season, a reason, or a lifetime. When you know which one it is, you will know what to do for that person."

I don't share my feelings with people who don't receive them in a caring and kind way. They have lost the right to hear what's on my mind and how I'm feeling, because they are not a safe outlet. By the way, you don't have to say that or explain things. You can just start to create a healthier distance to protect yourself.

And finally, it's also important to do something nice for yourself after you have been in a stressful situation. Go shopping; spend an afternoon alone; take a long, hot bath. Lean on your support. Practice strength. Don't let others rob you of your joy. Know your value and worth.

Anthony

By now, you've probably noticed that a lot of faith meeting therapy is talking about boundaries and balance, power and responsibility, fear and healthy relationships. Mental, physical, and spiritual health are connected. It all works together.

Stacy

And balance is key. There are always two sides to a coin. Clients often ask me what to do about some of their other important relationships. Because you cannot easily avoid them, two of the most challenging are toxic in-laws and employers. These two relationship types introduce a whole other level of difficulty because there are deeper issues to navigate, which makes it harder to distance yourself from someone or dump them.

When it comes to toxic in-laws, it's important to remind yourself that you would not have your partner if not for them. So if you reorient to a sense of appreciation that they raised your person, that might at least take away some of the frustration. Just keep in mind that it's usually better to let your mate deal with that in-law. Blood relatives have more influence and grace for dysfunction.

What if it's your boss? Frequently, a supervisor thinks that their position gives them permission to abuse power, and sometimes all we can do is find ways to minimize the damage. "Spectator mode," which is like the gray rock method, can help. Consider that you're simply a spectator in a difficult situation. Emotionally distance yourself and only respond with things like, "Okay, thank you. Yes, yes." Then leave it at the office. Especially if you need your job. If you don't need your job, you can begin to look for something else.

As we wrote this, the holidays were fast approaching. No other time of year brings up the topic of toxic relatives—those who insist on pushing buttons, who seem to know exactly how to get under our skin—like when we gather for Thanksgiving or Christmas. Sometimes we have to make up our mind to fly above it. (We don't have to discuss politics or religion at the dinner table.) A tennis match requires effort and participation from two people. You can always refuse to pick up a racquet and hit the ball.

About once a year I have a friend who comes for a holiday dinner. Whenever I find myself seated next to her, she talks nonstop, all criticisms and complaints, venting her opinion on everything. Boundaries for therapists can be a little like those in ministry. I do not mind people genuinely wanting my help, and I have a lot of grace and compassion for everyone, but having someone dump insults on me at a holiday dinner is something no one should have to endure.

Finally, in 2019, I decided I had done my time. I made sure to sit on the same side of the table as her, with two people between us, so she couldn't look me over and ask why I was wearing this outfit or suggest I cut back on dessert because my rolls were showing.

As we passed the vegetables around, she was leaning forward and back, craning her neck to see. "Where's Stacy?" she grumbled. "I can't see Stacy . . ."

Yes! I thought. *I am doing this every time.* And for the first time ever, I actually had a smile on my face connected to her. I felt so powerful!

She texted the day after to say,

Next year I'm sitting next to you! Ð

Saved by the pandemic, thanks be to God. And *no*, she is *not* sitting beside me next year!

Anthony

I get really frustrated when someone puts me in a situation where I have to speak up for myself. Even with practice and support it still makes me anxious, because I want them to be self-aware enough to not put me, or anyone, in that position. But I know that expectation is not realistic. Some people are amazing, healthy human beings who simply have blind spots—because they are exactly that, human beings.

Stacy

I get that completely. I also wish I wasn't put into situations where I have to speak up in this way. I have always tried to be the peacemaker, and I would much rather everybody just be calm and get along.

Anthony

Christians are supposed to be tolerant and forgiving, but where is the line between grace and enabling someone to treat you badly? I have a hard time with that one.

Stacy

Most of us do. I think the difference comes down to whether the other person is putting in a sincere effort. As long as they are trying, growing, and changing, offer grace. But grace comes with boundaries. God offers forgiveness, but actions have consequences. Behavior counts.

Grace in most relationships, to me, looks like this prayer: *God helps the helpless, for clearly, they cannot help themselves. Please give me strength and courage to deal with this dysfunctional person.*

I am not trying to change that person; as I always say, a person has to want to change. I'm not expecting anything. The best thing I can do is take that energy and work on changing myself while investing time and energy in those who are deserving of it.

In the intersection between faith and mental health, it's important to mention that most of us have been on both sides. Chances are, at some point, we have been guilty of toxic behaviors too.

Anthony

One Saturday afternoon, I was eating at Roscoe's House of Chicken and Waffles with both my sisters. I was telling them about this totally dysfunctional relationship I had gotten myself caught up in, and for once in my life, I wanted my big sisters to tell me what to do.

My oldest sister, Chrystal, took awhile to get her thoughts out, but once she did, she dropped bombs. "Anthony," she said, "if I was cooking a pot of your favorite soup, and accidently spilled a little bug spray in it, what would I need to do with that whole pot of soup? Could I just stir it in or tell you to eat around the poison? Or ignore it because it was just a little bit?"

I knew where she was going with that. Toxic is toxic. You can't eat around it. You've got to get rid of the soup.

Stacy

But let me ask from a therapist's perspective to someone of faith: What about grace and forgiveness?

Anthony

Matthew 18:21–22 says, "Peter came up and said to [Jesus], 'Lord, how often will my brother sin against me, and I forgive him? As many as seven times?' Jesus said to him, 'I do not say to you seven times, but seventy-seven times'" (ESV).

The Bible also says in Proverbs 20:3, "Avoiding strife is an honor for a person, but any fool will quarrel" (NASB). And Proverbs 14:7 instructs us to "stay away from fools" (NLT).

Yes, we are supposed to forgive, but it's important to avoid making excuses for people. God holds us accountable. Forgiveness comes at a cost, and even with God, there must be repentance and a true desire for change.

So there is grace and accountability. Once again, balance is the key.

Stacy

I believe God wants people to be free, not miserable and stuck. We should want the same for ourselves. A toxic relationship will tear you down. It can eat away your self-worth and self-esteem and damage your mental health.

If you're not ready for therapy yet, do whatever you can. Read self-help books, watch videos online, talk to trusted friends. Find ways to create distance, and work on your own issues. Maybe it's coming to counseling or joining a support group or starting an exercise program.

Start where you are, with what you have. Just the process of starting something is beneficial to emotional health. Sometimes it takes awhile to build up the strength to change.

Anthony

We could've written a whole book on dysfunctional relationships. It's a big concern for me and for a lot of people, I'm sure. I feel like we should pray after that one. Would you join me?

Father, we are grateful for our time together, for these hearts, these souls, these children of Yours who are represented here. We're thankful that You have given us community, to be able to talk openly about being better, being balanced, being more of what You've created and called us to be. I ask that You will show us the truth of what we need to do in our lives to create space for peace, space for wholeness, and space for mental clarity.

For the hearts who are hurting, who are lonely, I pray that You will guard them and help them feel Your presence come into their lives. That You would do that for all of us as we continue to tell the world how loving and kind You are, not only through words but also through actions.

We are grateful for You and that You have offered us relationship that is loving and true. In Your name we pray.

Amen. Amen. Amen.

—————— STACY'S TIPS TO HELP YOU GET STARTED

- **REFLECTION:** Evaluate your role in dysfunctional relationships. Do you continue to invest time and energy in people who are hurting you? Do you walk on eggshells when you are around them? Do you set boundaries and speak up when you are not being heard?

- **REALIZATION:** Get very clear about any role you are playing in getting hurt. If, for instance, they are throwing insults at you at holiday dinner, are you still sitting next to them, or did you get out of the way?
- **ACTION:** How can you refocus your life so you have more time and energy for yourself and those who lift you up instead of bringing you down? If you plan to continue to have dysfunctional relationships in your life, be sure you do the following:

  - Educate yourself about how the toxic person thinks and responds.
  - Find your voice. Speak up. Set boundaries.
  - Make sure that most of the other people in your life are positive and uplifting.
  - As a part of refocusing, make conscious efforts to spend time with and appreciate those who bring joy and peace into your life.

IF YOU CAN'T LIMIT PHYSICAL SPACE, LIMIT MENTAL SPACE.

ELEVEN

EXPERIENCE FORGIVENESS BY LETTING GO

Be kind and compassionate to one another, forgiving
each other, just as in Christ God forgave you.

EPHESIANS 4:32

Anthony

I love the gym and really enjoy getting in there as much as possible. There's nothing like working out with people who have the same goals and who are also great friends. Over time, I have developed calluses on my palms from steady lifting. Where before it was regular skin, the surface is now thick and hard. I have no feeling there when I press on them.

I was looking at these calluses one day when it occurred to me that they offer a good example of what happens to my heart when I don't put down the weight of unforgiveness. Calluses develop and I start to lose feeling.

These hard spots on my palms originally began to grow because of what I had been carrying. They were my body's way of shielding me from feeling the pain that can come from lifting something that heavy.

We have our feelings for a reason. They are there as an alert—a warning system to help us know what is good or bad for us. Continued unforgiveness makes the calluses on our hearts start to turn on us. Relentlessly holding on to the weight of unforgiveness inevitably becomes too much, and our calluses become thicker and thicker. Soon we lose feeling.

Stacy

Forgiveness means different things to different people, but in my view, forgiveness is making a conscious decision to take the feelings of resentment you have toward a person who has hurt you or harmed you in any way and letting that go. Forgiveness doesn't mean you forget. It doesn't mean you agree with what that person did or you make excuses for them. It is about showing mercy for someone who has caused you pain, whether they deserve it or not.

Forgiveness is something we do for our own good. Carrying resentment is like a poison inside, and over time, it can eat us alive. Forgiveness is an important step toward peace.

Anthony

I've realized that forgiving someone is choosing to put down emotional weight before it harms me. Like taking weight off the bar at the gym before I injure myself.

I used to carry so much locked up inside. Walking around with extra weight all the time is exhausting. Even though I knew all the scriptures and sermons, I could not seem to let any of it go.

The weight of unforgiveness will take over your whole life. You could be on a fancy vacation in Maui eating a dinner especially prepared for you by a private chef and be unable to enjoy it because your mind is still consumed by what someone did to you.

Stacy

That's why revenge plays such a big part in plotlines for film and TV. Revenge fantasies are very seductive. But revenge can actually get you in real trouble and brings no peace in the end. Only forgiveness can give you peace.

Holding on to anger, hatred, and offense keeps us stuck in the past and stuck on a loop, replaying the incident repeatedly in our minds. Forgiveness makes it so that you can step into the present and move forward.

Anyone who has ever experienced pain and disappointment from someone or something knows that small hurts are easier to let go than big hurts. Big hurts can impact our emotional, physical, and spiritual well-being. We can even get so caught up in the pain of our past that it becomes hard to live in the moment or plan for the future.

The Bible, or most any book on faith, talks about the importance of living in the moment and giving it our full attention (Isaiah 43:18–19).

Anthony

Colossians 3:13 says, "Bear with each other and forgive one another if any of you has a grievance against someone. Forgive as the Lord forgave you." That's a high call, to forgive like Jesus. The hard part is, how do you forgive without letting someone take advantage of you?

Stacy

It's so wonderful that Anthony has been fortunate to have a loving mom and dad. But I want to tell you about a client who has two emotionally abusive, toxic, neglectful parents. And even though she doesn't have contact with them anymore, she carries the anger from her childhood every day. This has caused her great pain and has affected her life in many areas.

She struggles to have intimate relationships because she can't stop venting about her family to anyone she dates. She's angry at work and with friends. I'm not discounting what she has been through or suggesting that she shouldn't be suffering from the pain of her past. But I do want her to get to a place where her anger and pain are not getting in the way of fulfillment and happiness. Forgiveness can help with that.

To forgive does not mean you open yourself up for abuse again. The last thing my client needs to do is let her parents back into her life. But most of us don't feel like regret and anger are something we can simply release. If we could let it go, we would. Those feelings have sunk their claws into us.

Sometimes we have to take a moment to ask, "Why did this person do this? Why did it happen?" Any level of understanding can help ease the pain. My client's parents both had abusive childhoods and never processed their upbringing, so they just passed it on to the next generation. That's not an excuse, but at least it's something of an explanation of why they behaved that way. As a matter of fact, as bad as they were, they both had parents who were even worse! They repeated the patterns they learned and actually believed that their abusive behavior was "good parenting."

Anthony

Stacy's guidance on forgiveness has helped me a lot. It's helped me forgive faster and not hold a grudge. To me, a grudge is like residue on the bottom of an oven—like when you're baking mac and cheese and it boils over and sticks to everything. Usually, I'll just leave it there and pray it magically disappears or burns away, but eventually it starts to stink.

Holding a grudge, even though the person might not be in your life anymore, is the same. It boils over and leaves gunk all over your life. Anytime you heat up, there will be smoke, and before long, it'll start to stink.

Even on the cross, in the middle of the worst heartbreak any person has known, Jesus said, "Father, forgive them, for they do not know what they are doing" (Luke 23:34). Jesus understood they were acting out of ignorance. God wanted to be close to us, and full forgiveness was what it took to make that happen.

Forgiveness offers that for us too. That is God's desire—for us to be emotionally, physically, and spiritually free. Anytime I am tempted to hold a grudge, I think about how the Lord has forgiven me.

Forgiveness isn't just setting someone else free. It sets you free too.

Stacy

Many research studies show how forgiveness leads to better physical and mental health. It eases depression and anxiety. It helps you sleep. It boosts your immune system.[5]

Let's not forget self-forgiveness. I work with a lot of people who will forgive others way before forgiving themselves. You can feel guilty and still forgive yourself for it anyway.

Anthony

The Evans men are a naturally thick people. If I let my body go unattended, it starts to lead me right toward the big-and-tall section of the department store. I have to remain conscious of my health at all times. But when I make the decision to get in shape, it always helps me feel better. Less stress on the joints, my blood pressure goes down, and energy levels go up.

In the same way, there are a lot of physical symptoms that come from not attending to your emotional health. I've felt my heart was racing or had headaches when I was allowing things in my life that were emotionally unhealthy. Often, unforgiveness is related to anxiety, depression, and countless other stress-induced ailments.

Just like physical health, attending to your emotional health and getting your emotions in shape isn't always easy. There's no magic shortcut, but it sure will make you feel better once it's done.

Stacy

Plus, when you begin to see results, the momentum grows and it gets easier and easier to stick to it.

Anthony

It's so amazing how our bodies and souls work together. But there's one more thing that I think is super important to remember. Though the act of forgiveness works, it's critical to recognize that some hurts are just too big for you to handle on your own. In some situations the path to forgiveness is only possible with God's help. If that's where you are, ask Him to work on your heart and help you find the healing power of forgiveness. This might be the time to ask Him to show you the right therapist to assist you on your journey.

In some cases, you might need the motivation to take the first step. There are so many references in the Bible we could mention here, but for now let's use Matthew 6:14: "If you forgive other people when they sin against you, your heavenly Father will also forgive you."

Let's say that someone stole $10,000 from you. I mean, that is a lot of money! You would be justified in being righteously angry.

Now, let's say that at the same time there was someone offering you $1 million, but the only way to get the one million would be to forgive and let go of the ten thousand. I don't know about you, but that would help me let go and forgive the other person fast. I would still have to work through the reality of what they did, but being focused on what I gained would help me move on.

Jesus says that He will forgive us when we forgive others. Listen, if you're like me, you've done a lot more to offend Jesus than you have other people. And in that, I would gladly forgive one, two, even fifty people to have Him freely pour His forgiveness and redemptive mercy all over my life.

Stacy

One million dollars would certainly be a great incentive to let something go, but since few of us will ever be so lucky, we need to find other incentives to help us let things go when we find ourselves holding on.

Since you know holding on to negative feelings causes internal suffering, allow your faith to guide you. Recognize that you have choices and control over how you think, feel, and behave, and choose inner peace as your incentive to let negativity go.

So I have a little confession to make. I often turn to music to help me escape painful lingering feelings. I like blasting one of Anthony's songs, but when it comes to forgiveness issues, I prefer to turn on that unforgettable tune from *Frozen* and belt out, "Let it go, let it go . . ."[6]

——————— STACY'S TIPS TO HELP YOU GET STARTED

- **REFLECTION:** Think about how holding on to your anger toward others has affected your life personally. Are you angry? Do you have obsessive thoughts? Is it affecting your relationships? Do you feel emotionally drained? Ask yourself what has been standing in the way of you setting yourself free.
- **REALIZATION:** Try to think about how and why the person who treated you badly acted that way. You do not need to excuse their behavior, but this might help explain it. Did they have a dysfunctional childhood? Were they having a bad day or week or year? Could it be a misunderstanding? Think about your own history. Have you ever offended or hurt someone? Did you have your reasons? Did you do it without even realizing it? Any place you can find empathy will help.
- **ACTION:** Work on building your forgiveness muscles by committing to stop thinking negative thoughts or expressing negative words about the person who hurt you. That doesn't mean you have to have

kind words or thoughts about the person; it's just about saying nothing at all, so you can begin to take the energy out of the experience. Also, as you think about people who have hurt you, practice forgiving those who have hurt you the least.

- Ask yourself if there have been any lessons or benefits from the pain you experienced and focus on those. For example, my client I discussed earlier in this chapter has promised herself that she will never abuse her own kids, so her children are benefiting from that decision.
- If you are struggling to forgive, have patience with yourself and get support from those you trust. Again, consider counseling if you need a safe, therapeutic place to process your pain.

FORGIVENESS DOESN'T JUST SET SOMEONE ELSE FREE. IT SETS YOU FREE TOO.

TWELVE

PROTECT YOUR PEACE, THEN LIVE IN IT

Guard your heart above all else, for it is the source of life.

PROVERBS 4:23 CSB

Anthony

The other night I was performing at an event in South Florida, and nothing was going right. Ideally I would have had plenty of rest and water, warmed up my voice, and done a sound check a few hours before the event. But life throws curveballs. Instead, flights were delayed. My driver got lost without cell reception. Logistics were crazier and more difficult due to the pandemic. Nothing was ideal.

I've been performing and doing ministry long enough that I have learned how to autocorrect on the fly. But I do know that if I don't guard my peace, those problems will get in my head, destroy my focus, and wreck the night. I don't have to hit a home run every time I'm up to bat. That's not realistic. I only have to get up each day and know that I'm doing the very best I can with what is right in front of me.

Though I've learned to find that balance in my career, I am constantly and consistently trying to apply that same balance to my emotional, spiritual, and mental life as well.

Stacy

Anthony is in a unique situation in that even if he's having a bad day, he has to get on a platform and be upbeat and inspirational. How do you get yourself back on track if you become sidetracked, especially when you feel that you have lost your peace?

Anthony

It depends on what I am facing. Usually, it starts with getting quiet and still. It's what I need to begin figuring out exactly what might be causing the problem.

I remember when I was a kid having trouble breathing because of my asthma. Dr. Denny would put a stethoscope on my chest and say, "Be quiet and take a deep breath, Anthony." That was what he needed to be able to hear my heart and lungs and to start getting to the root of the issue.

In the same way, I need to be quiet and take deep breaths to hear what is going on in my heart and to hear the Lord's voice. Whether that's sitting and doing nothing until my mind stops racing, going on a walk, or keeping a scripture in mind, I have to take the first step of being quiet and still. From there I can discern the source of the problem and figure out the steps that will bring me back to that center of peace.

I think I've also become more vulnerable as time has passed. If I am really struggling, I might confess that to family, friends, and sometimes even the audience I'm singing to. I've seen moments when God used that to cause a breakthrough in worship. A certain peace and comfort comes from sharing what you are going through with others instead of holding it in.

The Lord has blessed me with many things for which I'm so very grateful, but what I treasure most is the gift of peace. Peace is priceless. It simply cannot be purchased. But obtaining it does require work. What I had to learn the hard way is that no car, house, check, roaring applause, new outfit, or amount of Instagram likes is going to give me a true and sustained peace in my heart and mind.

The pathway to true peace opens up when you realize that it is not predicated on what is happening externally. Peace comes when you trust the anchor of your faith, even in the storm. Yes, storms can create fear, questions, and uncertainty, but when you completely and totally trust your anchor, a peace settles deep inside you.

Discovering, experiencing, and protecting our peace is one of the major steps toward internal health. Stacy taught me that peace has to be fought for and helped me develop a plan that works for me.

Stacy

One of my key therapeutic rules is that we are all responsible for protecting our peace. That's not a passive process. Toxic people, guilt, unrealistic expectations, overthinking, overdosing on technology—we need to be aware of what's happening in and around us and protect ourselves, because all these things can steal away our peace. Of course, there are also times when our emotions can sneak up on us. Like weeds taking over a yard, stressful and unwanted situations can creep in until they take over every aspect of our lives.

Some people go to church and assume they will automatically find peace because of their participation in that process. But unless you are carrying peace on the inside, even the good things happening externally may not be able to reach you.

Anthony

I did that for years. Obviously, I'm a church kid, and I was there all the time. But on the inside I was still a wreck. It didn't matter how good the worship service was or if the preacher delivered the sermon of the year. On top of that, trying to pretend like you're fine when your heart is troubled only makes the pain worse. It's like having a sprained ankle and trying to walk without a limp.

Now don't get me wrong; church is very important and something we shouldn't ignore. But you would be surprised how many people sitting in church pews are just as broken and confused and anxious and depressed as those who don't even attend. Peace is not automatically downloaded into your soul just because you walk through the church door and sing a verse and chorus of "See a Victory." Many a Sunday, I would sit in church and be miserable, even though I was singing and praying and doing all the things I thought would bring peace. Then I was right back in the mud of guilt and shame. *What's wrong with me? Why can't I pray through it? Why can't I get it to work for me?*

Internal peace was not my first focus. I was looking to external experiences rather than my own heart, soul, and mind. Jesus told us that the kingdom of God is not something that can be easily observed. It's not in a song or sermon or even a book. The kingdom of God is inside you (Luke 17:20–21).

In Psalm 119, King David talked about hiding God's Word in his heart (v. 11). I believe that the Spirit of God gives you peace, and that starts on the inside. External things cannot do that.

The hard truth is that the accumulation of material things can make the lack of peace worse. I remember going on a trip, thinking that distance from my circumstances would fix things. As I sat on the beach and cried, I realized that you cannot run from yourself. The issue was inside me. In that moment I realized that until I did the work, I was going to continue to feel anxious no matter where I was or what new thing I acquired.

Stacy

Notice that many people say, "Rest in peace," and yet we rarely hear people say, "Live in peace."

Anthony

The only way to rest is to live in peace. We can rest in peace on this side of heaven too.

Stacy

With a foundation of peace, you are going to be happier, more productive, and have a better life overall. This is possible even in unpeaceful times. The pandemic, civil unrest, and other external stressors that are out of our control all make it difficult to maintain peace within ourselves. This is why it becomes critically important to manage our regular, daily sense of inner peace as we monitor our emotional health and sense of harmony.

Anthony

We can't necessarily change everything that's happening around us. For instance, it's about three hundred miles from Dallas to Galveston. My speedometer goes to 140. I could make it to the beach in a little over two hours if I drove that fast from my house to the Gulf of Mexico. Wouldn't that be great? Like, the most fun and productive trip ever.

But even if I could avoid all the patrol cars, roads have potholes and construction zones. I can't run at full capacity because if I did, I'd tear up my vehicle or hurt myself trying to avoid road hazards. Sometimes you can attempt to repave the road you are on or even change your route. But the best idea is to slow down.

Stacy

Some days you simply need to stop, turn the car around, and go home. Simplify your life. See what you can do to make things easier.

The Serenity Prayer says, "God, grant me the serenity to accept the things I cannot change, courage to change the things I can, and wisdom to know the difference."

Carrying on with the pothole-and-road-construction analogy, the condition of the road may be out of your power to change. So you change your focus to the things that are within your control. That takes wisdom and insight.

We are responsible for our physical, mental, and spiritual health. We eat right, exercise, and focus on trying to get a good night's rest. In the same way, we work on keeping our mental and spiritual muscles toned. Involvement in a community of faith, introspection, and prayer are all important—and part of that is good counsel and guidance as well.

Continuing on from our discussion in the last few chapters, it's worth taking a good hard look at the people in your life who disrupt your peace. It may be a close friend or even a sibling. You might love this person dearly, but every time you are around them, you can feel your peace slipping away and anxiety or anger or frustration taking its place.

In terms of protecting your peace, you must minimize those people's access to your life. Sometimes you must cut them out completely. That is not an easy thing to do.

Anthony

At times it can also be necessary to "reposition people in the room" of your life. If I were a Broadway actor and there was someone in the front row who kept being disruptive and pulling me out of character, what would happen? They would be asked to be quiet. If they were again disruptive, they would be asked to move. If they did it again, even from a new seat farther back in the room, they would be asked to leave.

This is exactly what I've adopted in my real life for anyone who is disruptive and pulls me out of the character that God wants me to be. Without fear, I put some distance between myself and them. I have learned that once that seat is empty, someone who wants nothing other than to see and support my staying in character without disruption will fill it. And what's the main reason that person who promotes peace hasn't been there all along? It's because their seat was taken!

Ultimately we should limit the access we give to people who pull us out of our God-given character. That sounds unchristian in a way, and I'm not saying we should become selfish or refuse to help those in need. We are called to endure and be patient with one another (Ephesians 4:2). But again, balance is important for walking in love and peace.

Stacy

Setting good boundaries is also essential to a peaceful life. People can be messy. They will test your limits. You know that saying, "Good fences make good neighbors"? Healthy relationships have clear boundaries. You know where the lines are set.

So, yes, that requires balance, and the key is being aware and present in the moment. Just deal with what is in front of you. Often we experience what therapists call *anticipatory anxiety*, where we are borrowing problems from the future and worrying about things that haven't even happened yet.

One way to protect your peace is to simply deal with whatever is right in front of you. Try not to get caught up in yesterday or tomorrow.

Anthony

To that point, I have another house story for you. I love Los Angeles. The hills and beaches and winding roads. And the weather is spectacular. Southern California rarely sees rain. But Los Angeles is not necessarily the safest place to own a home. Most everybody here has bars on their windows, something you don't see much back in Texas. I hate the way bars on windows look. It feels like I'm living in prison. So I did not put any on my home.

Then life in LA started getting crazier—riots, thefts, home invasions on the rise. My mind is overactive as it is, so I broke down and put bars on all my windows, nice ones that at least somewhat matched the style. Bars are expensive, and it's not something I wanted to do, but I had them installed because it helps me sleep and live in peace. It still looks ugly to me from the street, but peace is more important than perception.

Some of us need to put up some bars to protect our minds, our hearts, and our relationship with God. Bars don't mean you keep everyone out. There are still doors. The bars mean that you keep out those who are uninvited.

Stacy

Home has to be a place of peace. We all need a safe place to rest and recharge. You might give certain trusted people a key to your house. They know and respect your boundaries. But for most relationships, we need fences, locks, and like Anthony said, sometimes even bars.

I believe this is an important topic for people of faith, because we want to be benevolent and available to help—but how do we keep others from trampling on our lives? Very few of us are naturally good at setting boundaries, especially those of us who are compassionate and want to be of service to others. How do we live with open hands while protecting our peace?

Anthony

Let me share a couple of Bible verses that resonate with that topic. Philippians 4:7 says, "The peace of God, which transcends all understanding, will guard your hearts and your minds in Christ Jesus."

Proverbs 12:20 tells us that "those who plan peace have joy" (ESV). There are so many verses about peace throughout Scripture. The bottom line is that there *is* a peace that will surpass all understanding, but it is up to us; we have to take hold of that peace ourselves. In the same way that physical fitness doesn't just happen, there's work and commitment involved. The Bible tells us that peace requires a plan if we are to live in it.

In addition, the pursuit of peace is more about consistency than intensity. Daily making the right decisions, even small ones, will lead you to your goal.

Stacy

I like that idea from Proverbs that people who plan peace will have joy. That's a good verse to tie into what we are talking about in this chapter. Peace is not some feeling of calm that randomly washes over you. The pursuit of peace must be intentional; but again, I believe God meets us in our efforts.

Anthony

You know that peace that passes all understanding? I can truly say I have that in my life. Given the circumstances of the last few years, I had no idea that being consistent in how I fought for and protected my peace would end up with me writing this book with Stacy. As strained and stressed as I was before, all hell broke loose. I never thought I could make it through that much loss. All I can say is I did the work. I did the best I could, and God met me there. Somehow, miraculously, I am living in peace. At least I am today.

Stacy

Today is a good start.

Anthony

There's a scene in *The Lion King* where Simba is trying to roar to keep the hyenas away, but when he opens his mouth, not much sound comes out. His "roar" in the moment wouldn't scare a bunny rabbit away, much less a hyena. He's doing all he can, but his enemies only laugh at him.

Finally, he tries again. Simba pulls back, takes a deep breath, and lets out a monster roar that could be heard for miles. Like thunder crashing, his voice shakes the air. The hyenas retreat in fear. The camera pans out to reveal that Simba's father saw his attempt and came to stand over him, to roar above him. He saw that he was giving his all and joined in.[7]

When I do my best, I feel like God steps in to roar on my behalf. He immediately and intensely lets my enemies know they are messing with the wrong one. He reminds them that they have no power because He's covering me.

Stacy

So what kind of things can you expect to feel inside when you know you are at peace with your life? I've walked through this with Anthony, and I think he's got some great experiences to share on that front.

Anthony

I like to be busy and working—everything moving fast. Sometimes I've been guilty of staying busy just so I don't have to think about my current reality. One of the questions I had to ask myself was, *Am I okay just being with myself and not having to do something to distract myself from all the chaos that's going on in my heart?*

So one way I knew I was gaining peace was that I started feeling more okay with being quiet and still. In the past, if I had gotten still, I would start to worry and my mind would race and work me up until I felt crazy. The process of therapy helped me understand that this was not God's intention for me. He didn't want me to live like that. But I have to partner in the work. I make investments in bettering myself.

For years I had an amazing physical trainer—I'm the kind of person who needs an extra push and some accountability. His name is JP, and his nickname for me was Eeyore, that sad donkey from *Winnie the Pooh*. Eeyore was always worried, always gloomy, certain that trouble was just around the corner all the time.

You know what? JP was right. There I was sharing God's truth and His faithfulness through worship music, while at the same time walking around under a dark cloud.

But when I started doing the work of being quiet and still, setting good boundaries, living in the present, and keeping my faith and trust in God, Eeyore stopped coming around. It wasn't magic, and it didn't happen overnight, but I slowly started to get out from under that cloud. The weight began to lift, and when that happened it encouraged me to keep moving forward.

I remember coming in for my normal workout one day and JP saying, "Hey, it's been a while since I've seen Eeyore! What changed?"

In that moment it felt exactly like when someone says, "Hey, have you been working out? You look different and healthier." The progress was noticeable. That is what the pathway to peace looks like—small steps that end up changing the shape of your soul, for the better.

My life is far from perfect now, and I still have moments when I slip into Eeyore mode. It's like that saying, "I'm not where I need to be, but I am not where I used to be either." I still have bad days and I still have struggles. But the lows are not so low these days.

In John 16:33 Jesus said, "I have told you these things, so that in me you may have peace. In this world you will have trouble. But take heart! I have overcome the world." Jesus was saying, *It's going to be hard. We live in a fallen world. Bad things happen. People are imperfect. I've told you all these things so you can have peace.*

When I lost my mom, it was the worst thing ever. *Worst* doesn't even do it justice—to watch your mother slowly die with all the loss of dignity and sickness and pain. I felt so helpless and lost. In that moment I had to trust God's Word. And honestly, that is the only reason I am standing strong today—trusting that, even though the weight of sadness felt unbearable, even though there was trouble, I could still take heart and have peace. God has overcome the world and all its troubles.

I begged God to heal my mom. We all did. Great prayers of faith went up around the world. But He said no to the way we were asking Him to heal her. His version of healing was for her to be with Him. That could have destroyed my peace. But you see, God's no was also a yes. She is now in perfect peace.

When you trust that God has overcome all troubles and that He has the final word, it will substantially change your perspective and your sense of peace for the better.

I promise you that.

———— STACY'S TIPS TO HELP YOU GET STARTED

- **REFLECTION:** What does peace look like for you? It can be different for each of us. Some of us find peace walking in nature, others find peace watching a good TV show, and others find peace through worship. Ask yourself: Who or what in your life robs you of your peace? It is important to examine all areas that affect your peace so you can begin to create changes.
- **REALIZATION:** Begin to realize the importance of inner peace. Assess what you can control and what you cannot control about your own peace.
- **ACTION:** Commit to doing the following:

  - Engage in daily activities that provide you peaceful moments.
  - Set boundaries with those who disturb your peace. If that is someone you live with, make sure you

communicate with them about what changes need to take place.

- If you are dealing with a person who refuses to work on changing or who does not respect your boundaries, you may need to minimize your interactions or end them altogether. Or you might need to use buffers during stressful moments. These buffers would likely be other people who can join you so you aren't alone with a toxic person. A buffer might also be an activity; something like sitting at a ball game, a movie, or a church event can allow you both to focus on where you are instead of on each other.

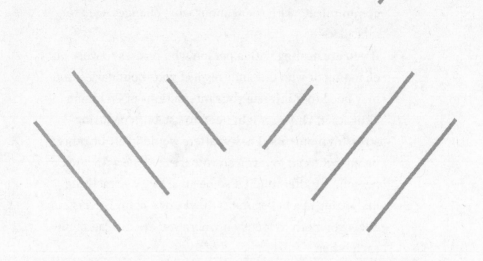

THE ONLY WAY TO REST

IS TO LIVE IN PEACE.

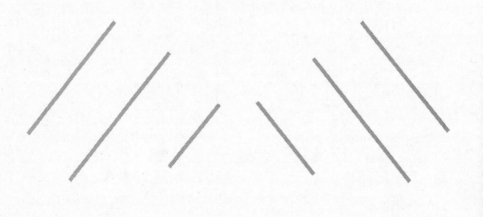

THIRTEEN

THE SEVEN KEYS TO HEALTHY RELATIONSHIPS

*Make every effort to add to your faith goodness; and to
goodness, knowledge; and to knowledge, self-control;
and to self-control, perseverance; and to perseverance,
godliness; and to godliness, mutual affection; and to
mutual affection, love.*

2 PETER 1:5–7

Anthony

A couple of summers ago, I was on vacation at a ranch in Colorado. The
week started off with a horse-drawn hayride. Because of my love for
horses, I asked the wrangler if I could sit up front with him.

In true Western style, two huge Belgian horses were all harnessed up
and ready to go. We were only going a mile down the road, but these two
beautiful giants looked like they were ready to trek for days across the

open plains. More than twenty of us jumped onboard the wagon, ready to enjoy the crisp mountain air.

Early into the ride, I noticed that Joe, the wrangler, kept pushing Smith, the Belgian on the left. His partner to the right was named Wesson.

He would take his rein and send a wave of leather out to the backside of Smith, over and over. When I asked him what was going on, Joe replied, "Well, Smith is notorious for letting Wesson do all the work. He has made a habit of coasting and plays the part of pulling his share without actually doing it. He's become well aware that if he *doesn't* do his job, Wesson will do it for him."

As I leaned in, Joe continued, "What has happened over the past few years is that Wesson, because he's doing most of the work, has started to develop arthritis in his knees and hocks. He was never made to pull the load for two."

That's when it hit me. Not unlike Wesson, some of us have allowed ourselves to be hitched to people who don't pull their share of the load. And in turn, we are the ones who end up getting injured. The only difference between these horses and us in this analogy is that we have the *choice* to take off what attaches us to people like this.

Stacy

No doubt, a lot of giving people end up drawing in those who only want to take. All too often it's the generous soul who ends up getting hurt. And yet the goal for all of us is to have healthy, uplifting, and fulfilling relationships!

Anthony

And faith can make it harder. Some of us allow our beliefs to make us think we are supposed to give and give and give, ignore our own needs, and suffer for the kingdom.

The Bible gives a lot of warnings about being unequally yoked

(2 Corinthians 6:14). I believe part of what that means is that we have faith-based relationships with a healthy measure of give-and-take. Things get unequal when one person is doing all the work and the other can just coast.

Stacy

That's right. Interestingly enough, some people simply fall into difficult relationships, while others seek them out, thinking that they might be fun or edgy. Didn't nearly every one of us go through some form of that in our teenage years? As life passes, most of us live and learn, while others get stuck in a rut and return to unhealthy relationships time and time again. Maybe it's a way to protect our hearts by only engaging in empty, dead-end relationships. Some fear being able to measure up, so they aim low.

And then you have others who have been hurt so badly, they don't risk getting into a relationship at all. Some of my clients will often admit, "I don't have any real friends or anybody I can talk to."

"Do you try to meet new people?" I ask. "Do you put yourself out there?"

Many of them do not. They are literally hiding from life, growing frustrated, giving up. "There are no good people out there anymore," they will complain.

Yes, there are. But we must work on being able to meet and receive those good people and believe that we are worth it.

We discussed toxic relationships earlier, but I want to focus on healthy relationships as well. Over the years of working as a therapist, I've developed seven keys that I believe indicate quality, healthy relationships. If they seem like common sense, that's because they are fairly intuitive. But because it's often challenging to think clearly when you're dealing with strong emotions, it's best to have some tips and tools readily available. (Also note that you won't find these repeated in the practical tips at the end of the chapter—there's more for you there.)

Anthony

Y'all get out your highlighters. These keys have helped me so much.

Stacy

Key number one: the foundation of every good relationship is respect.

Disrespect is bad on every level. It hurts not only the relationship but also the individuals. Respectful behavior is anything from being considerate of another person's feelings to how we listen and speak to one another.

Anthony

If you give respect, you should be shown respect in return. Even if it's uncomfortable, I try to get boundaries out on the table early into a relationship and do that in the most honest and gracious way possible. Things get so much better when you can talk about what bothers you. Otherwise, mistrust and resentment can build up in your head to be this giant issue. Relationships require maintenance and investment, but with the right people it's more than worth it.

Stacy

A lot of disrespect is done unintentionally. But how would you know you were being disrespectful unless it was communicated? I have some good friends who I haven't seen in a long time because they don't live near me, and I don't feel comfortable traveling during the pandemic. Well, they made plans for a trip to Hawaii six months from now and didn't include me. That stung. Who knows how I'll feel half a year from now? I'd like to at least be asked.

I FaceTimed them to let them know I was hurt. They apologized, explained they thought I might not want to go, and we talked it out. Imagine if I hadn't made the effort to communicate. That could build up into a big ugly ball of anger and bitterness. We've all lost friends from the confusion that comes with miscommunication. (See key number six.)

If you go in with good intentions and an open mind, things can usually be worked out. Don't accuse; just talk about your own feelings and be willing to listen to the other side as well. There is always another side.

Anthony

Some people love to get defensive and pop off, but I've found that most scenarios can be defused with mature conversations.

Stacy

Key number two: quality relationships are marked by loyalty and trust.

If you can't trust someone, how can you connect? How can you enjoy their company? Walls of suspicion close off a person's heart and ability to connect.

We should invest our time and energy in people who have our backs. That doesn't mean we don't reach out to troubled people. But I do not believe we are called into deep relationships with dysfunction either. Our relationship with God is built on loyalty and trust, and that should be our blueprint for relationships with others as well.

On Instagram I will sometimes put out an opportunity for people to ask questions. Recently someone asked, "Do you think that dishonest and untrustworthy people can change?"

Of course I do. I wouldn't be in this business if I didn't believe people had the power to change. And Anthony and I would not be lending our voices to this book if we didn't believe it was possible.

Anthony

As weird as this might sound, I do think that we define relationships at times the same way I look at cars. I can't remember the last time I looked under the hood of a car I was about to purchase. But why would I not do that when the engine is what is going to get me to my desired destination?

With friendships, the most important characteristics are under the surface. Fun and laughs are amazing exterior qualities, but loyalty and trust are the engine that will get you to your destination. For sure they are the true benefits that come from real friendship.

Stacy

Key number three: people you are in a relationship with should make you feel like a priority.

The other person should not downplay your emotions or opinions or your time. You are a priority in their life, and they should feel like a priority in yours.

I have a client who has been in a relationship with a man who won't see her on the weekends.

Anthony

Uh . . . Big. Red. Flag.

Stacy

Though it's definitely suspicious, there may be a reasonable explanation. Talk about it. But if not? There's something fishy about someone who wants to be in a relationship but will not see you on Friday, Saturday, or Sunday.

My question to her was, "Do you feel like a priority in his life?"

Also, she's not allowed to go to his house. Never been.

Anthony

Oh, Lord. Can you please put this girl on speakerphone right now?

Stacy

And the more you hear this story, the more red flags you can see.

But trust is not just for romantic situations. Do you feel like a priority at work? With family? With your friends? Everybody wants to feel special.

Anthony

I think that segues nicely into the fourth key.

Stacy

Key number four: healthy relationships are marked by loving and caring gestures.

It could be a compliment or gift or taking over someone's household tasks for the week, or the simple act of telling someone how much you appreciate having them in your life.

Anthony

I am a loving-gesture kind of person. No apologies. With Stacy's help, I came to a place where I now understand and accept that this is just how God made me. Like she said, people need to know they are special and that you think about them.

Just today, I was on the phone with one of my closest friends. He recently got engaged, so he was talking a hundred miles per hour about everything that's going on in his life right now. After about ten minutes, he took a breath. "Oh my gosh, Anthony. I am so sorry," he said. "How are you doing?"

He realized that he had been talking nonstop and hadn't checked in with me.

"I'm good," I laughed. "Everything's good. Keep talking."

I've had friends in the past who never would have even thought about slowing down to check on how I'm doing. Everybody's had a friend like that, right? They only want to talk and never listen. And if you're a Christian you might be thinking, *Oh well, that's okay. It's not about me.*

No shade to Rick Warren, but if it's all about their wants and needs and happiness and never about yours, it is never going to work.

Stacy

Key number five: the other person's happiness and comfort should be equal to your own and vice versa.

Anthony gave us a good example. His newly engaged friend needed more time in that moment, so Anthony offered him ten uninterrupted minutes. I'm sure if Anthony needed to talk, he would get the same.

That's not the same as keeping score—because that's a key for dysfunction. Equal time and effort is more of a sense of fairness. We help each other. Sometimes one person needs more than the other, but then the pendulum swings back in the other direction when the other person is in need. We carry each other through. There is no score. Again, we return to the principle of balance.

Anthony

Keeping score reminds me of 1 Corinthians 13:4–5: "Love is patient, love is kind. It does not envy, it does not boast, it is not proud. It does not dishonor others, it is not self-seeking, it is not easily angered, it keeps no record of wrongs." God is giving us keys to a healthy relationship right there.

If you are a priority, the busiest person in the world will find time for you. At the risk of sounding like I am name-dropping, Kirk Franklin has been that kind of friend to me. We've been like family since I was about twenty years old. Kirk called my mother "Mama Lo."

I like to stay busy, but Kirk is on a whole different level. Think hurricane. Yet he still consciously makes time to check in with me, to ask how I am doing. It may be only five minutes, like we'll both be running through airports on different coasts, and I'll get a FaceTime from Kirk.

"Anthony, how are you?" he'll ask. "What's going on in your life? I love you, little brother."

Stacy

I would rather have five minutes of a friend's undivided attention than an hour where they are scattered and focused on nine other things besides me.

The Golden Rule is something to think about—do unto them as you'd have them do unto you—but we must take into consideration that person's personality. I have friends and family members who never call, but they're not phone people. I have other family members and friends who call too much, and then I can't get them off the phone.

Again, it comes down to equal effort without keeping score. Human behavior is not an exact science. Grace and understanding go both ways.

Anthony

I've had to learn the art of weighing out the nuances of each friendship that matters to me and giving the grace and understanding necessary to maintain them.

Stacy

Key number six: healthy relationships have good communication.

We've already discussed this a bit. Actually, all these topics and tips bleed one into another because that's the way healthy, living things grow. It all works together.

Regarding communication, let's get to the foundation of what it is and isn't.

Communication isn't measured by how much conversation you have.

Some people simply aren't big talkers. It's more the ability to talk about important issues, to resolve problems, to let each other know how you feel about things. It's not rolling your eyes or giving someone the silent treatment or employing any sort of passive-aggressive strategies to express what's on your mind. Although those things are still a form of communication, they are not the healthy or productive kind. Sometimes good communication is about being conscious of how, when, and why one communicates while working through issues, connecting, sharing, praising, and so forth.

Anthony

We have biological family, and then we have what I call our chosen families—the friends we have made and keep close, who we look to for support. I am thankful I get to lean on both.

The dynamic is different because with biological family, if I didn't talk to my sister for three years and I needed her, I know she would be there. But with my chosen family and my friends, that foundation of equal effort and open communication is important to keep things flowing well. We listen to each other with understanding.

Ecclesiastes 4:10 says, "If either of them falls down, one can help the other up. But pity anyone who falls and has no one to help them up."

I like Proverbs 27:17 too: "As iron sharpens iron, so one person sharpens another."

Stacy

Key number seven: maintain a sense of positivity.

That doesn't mean every moment is sunny and bright but more that you know that person is cheering you on. They want the very best in life for you.

All relationships have a measure of complaining and judgment, but overall, we want a sense of positivity over the negative. You need to enjoy each other's company. Spending time together shouldn't be a drain.

Anthony

I avoid negativity because it's too easy for me to get sucked into that mind-set. I refuse to let anyone pull me down. I will stop the conversation and just give them a look that says, *I heard that, and I'm not messing with it. We are not going to go there.*

Jesus was not a pushover, you know. I think that it's okay to carry that energy. In fact, I've found that some people appreciate being checked. I know I need it too.

Stacy

Get to know what's important to you and what bothers you. Even if you have to dismiss it in the moment. Let's say you are on the phone with one of your parents and they begin to complain or criticize. Maybe in the moment you have to tolerate it, but I believe it's important to pause once the call is over and say to yourself, *You know what? I don't like that. It bothers me.*

I mention that because I have so many clients whose parents wear them out with complaining. Just because you endure the behavior doesn't mean you endorse it. And for the record, the same applies to friends and romantic partners; many of them can wear a person out with complaints too!

Happiness within a relationship is hard to define. Not only is each relationship different, but within each relationship, each person defines happiness in an individual way. Some people view happiness as a peaceful, conflict-free life. For others, happiness involves a tremendous amount of fun, great conversation, or lots of laughter. Whatever your definition, it directly correlates to your expectations, desires, and needs—and those things can change over time.

What holds constant are seven specific behaviors and attributes that, in my experience, can almost guarantee the likelihood of long-term suc-cess and happiness in a relationship.

———— STACY'S TIPS TO HELP YOU GET STARTED

- **REFLECTION:** Spend some time thinking about your most important relationships. What is healthy? Unhealthy? What parts make you happy? Unhappy? What do you wish could change? What is your part in each relationship's successes and failures?
- **REALIZATION:** Relationships take ongoing investment and effort, and no relationship is perfect. Now that you have reflected, take a clear and honest look at what you think can change and what cannot. For example, your partner's snoring may not be changeable, but they can change leaving crumbs under the covers.
- **ACTION:** Commit to working on your relationship from your end.

  - What can *you* do to make things better?
  - Next, have a talk with the other person—let them know what you are working on improving and ask them if they have anything to add to your list of things to change. This should help set the tone for you to ask them what they might want to improve, and you can add to their list.

LOYALTY AND TRUST ARE THE ENGINE THAT WILL GET YOU TO YOUR DESTINATION.

| FOURTEEN |

GROW THROUGH
GRIEF AND LOSS

The LORD is close to the brokenhearted; he rescues those whose spirits are crushed.

PSALM 34:18 NLT

Anthony

If you know our family or maybe read our book *Divine Disruption*, you know the Evanses lost eight loved ones in two years and then went straight into a worldwide pandemic. We went through a lot of grief. Not only the loss of my cousin, aunt, uncles, grandfather, and mom, but grieving the loss of freedoms and career—life as we knew it before the virus spread and locked down the entire planet. It felt like grief with a side of grief, with grief on ice to wash it down.

Stacy

Grief is a part of life, but that much grief is a lot for any family.

Anthony

Before all that happened, I knew what Psalm 34:18 said about God being close to those whose hearts are broken. I can now say that I know it is true because I've lived through it. In the worst of times, God was so close.

Stacy

The Evans family has absolutely proven it true! But grief is a complicated emotion, and different people experience it in different ways.

We can grieve many things—the loss of a loved one or of a relationship, of hopes and dreams, a career. Some feel numb or heartbroken while others experience loss physically, struggling to eat or sleep. It can also look like chest pains, anxiety, or migraines.

Grief usually comes in waves. Some days you feel okay, like the worst just might be over. And then it hits you in an entirely different way. Grief is as old as time, yet always new.

I think we all have experienced a collective grief with the pandemic.

Anthony

It seems like everybody lost something. Time, money, the ability to get together with family and friends, or to simply eat out in a restaurant. Two years later, I still feel crazy. My whole life was getting on planes, singing, traveling, one event to the next—all that was snatched away.

Stacy

Most of us were affected mentally, socially, and financially. I had to start seeing clients online. Technology is wonderful, but the experience is just not the same as connecting in person.

I don't know what you did with your pandemic misery, but I learned to bake bread. I have a little sourdough starter that my niece gave me, and she was checking on me. "Are you feeding it?" she would ask. I made about ten loaves of sourdough bread. After my family started requesting other types of bread—wheat, white, rye—I finally stopped making bread.

Anthony

Some people learned to make bread in lockdown misery, and I learned to eat it. I can't leave the house, and nobody can see me? Bring on the biscuits . . .

Stacy

There are different degrees of grief, but loss is loss. Anything that is important to you will be grieved once it is gone. I always say that grief is a sign of the intensity of the love. The more you love, the more you will grieve, and the more you grieve, the more you loved. Again, there is no consolation in comparing your loss with someone else's.

Anthony

What can you do when a loss just feels too heavy and hard to take?

Stacy

First of all, it's important to know that when you are grieving, you're grieving not only what you have lost but also how your life has been changed. If it's the loss of a person, you are in pain but also thinking about the space they have left behind.

Anthony

I felt that when my mother passed. My mom was the one who kept it all together behind the scenes, family and ministry too. She was such a huge presence, and her fingerprints are everywhere on our lives. From family events, making sure my dad looked good at all times, to her calling to check on me and saying, "Now, Banto, how are *you* doing?" (Banto is what she called me.) Every day I not only grieve the loss of my mom, I also feel that empty space.

But I, along with my siblings and father, am determined to carry on her legacy.

Stacy

That's another tip—find ways to carry on the legacy, and build a legacy of your own. Do things that matter. Be intentional. Make an impact. Leave something good in this world.

I do public service not just for legacy but because that's where I get my sense of fulfillment. One of my friends said, "Are you trying to fill a football stadium for your funeral with people you have helped?"

The question threw me off, and I had to think a minute. "Yes," I finally replied. "If I can fill a football stadium when I die, I'll know that I'd accomplished something good."

I mean, maybe it's the football stadium of a very small private school, but still.

My friend suggested that it could be a bring-a-friend funeral and whoever filled the most seats would get a piece of my inheritance. Kind of like a raffle.

I'm adding a little bit of levity to this chapter on grief, because even in pain we all need a little relief. But I should say this: bring-a-friend funeral is only a joke. You absolutely don't need to do that when I pass!

Anthony

Okay, that's funny, but I don't want to even think about that!

Stacy

Well, I don't need a whole football stadium. A small concert hall would be just fine. Isn't it strange how we can be so nonchalant and comical about our own funerals, yet the thought of losing someone close to us is still devastating?

Either way, it's important to think about the legacy of someone you have lost. My grandmother was a major influence in my life—like a second mother to me. She was always in the kitchen baking something wonderful, so every year, around the holidays, my daughters and I make little cookie plates using her recipes.

I didn't think about it until now, but that's probably one of the reasons I baked bread during the pandemic. I was sad and afraid and wanted to feel loved and safe again. So I baked.

Anthony

My mom is from South America, so the Evans family holidays were always filled with all these wild flavors. Shortly before my mom died, Priscilla made a video of her cooking and sharing the recipes of her favorite meals. I walked into our kitchen last Christmas and got a whiff of all those Caribbean spices, and heard the pressure cooker's *rattle* and *hiss*. Then, I heard my mother's voice, closed my eyes, and for just a moment, I was home.

Dad came from the living room to the kitchen. "It feels like your mom's here," he said with a smile.

She *was* there with us, because we determined to keep her legacy alive, to celebrate all that she was and still is through her children and grandkids—through all the lives that she touched. There's something about preserving her essence that helps with the grief. Even though the tears were flowing that Christmas morning, I still had a smile on my face and peace in my heart. In that sense, Mommy will never leave us. She will always be here, until we meet her face-to-face again.

Psalm 126:6 says, "Those who go out weeping, carrying seed to sow, will return with songs of joy." My mother's passing broke me, but she gave us so many seeds. Planting those seeds brings me joy, whether it's cooking a batch of pepper pot, or treating people with love and respect, or simply making sure Dad's hair looks right before he goes on stage.

The grief remains, but there is peace and joy as well.

Stacy

My grandmother's house always smelled like onions because she cooked so much. Whenever I cut onions, I think of her. Now, onions aren't considered to have a pleasant smell, but I love it because it reminds me of her and it takes me back home.

It doesn't matter what you have lost or what you are grieving; take time to feel your feelings, otherwise they will sneak up when you least expect it. People who fail to grieve are eventually affected by their stuffed-away feelings. It's just a matter of time.

Some clients say to me, "I'm afraid if I ever let myself start crying, I won't stop."

Nobody cries forever. You only have so many tears before you exhaust yourself. Better messy on the outside than keeping it all in.

Anthony

Stacy and I both have referenced the loss of a loved one, but we know that grief comes from all forms of loss. Some of us are grieving the loss of jobs, finances, or health. During the pandemic, I had to grieve and deal with the loss of work. For twenty years all I've known is traveling and singing for a living. For a year, I didn't do it one time.

I had to really sit myself down and deal with my identity and with the question, "What am I going to do now?" I didn't know how I was going to get through it.

Stacy

When it comes to grief and loss and the life changes that come along for the ride, don't expect yourself to be okay. In other words, don't put expectations on your emotions. You know what the word *amen* means? *So be it.* Let it be. Don't try to fight or push your emotions away. Our emotions are there for a reason.

Earlier today I was working with a woman who mentioned her ex-husband from seven years ago, and when she did, she got tears in her eyes. "I don't know what is wrong with me," she said. "My ex is a horrible, narcissistic person, and I am so much better off without him."

"Yes, but you still have feelings for him, don't you?" I asked.

"Yes," she admitted. "He was terrible for me. But I loved him dearly."

I let her know that it was okay to grieve the good times they shared together. Nobody is all bad, right? There is good in most relationships, and the loss of the good parts can cause us to feel sad.

Grief is a challenging emotion. We're not going to figure out a way to go around it. My client felt bad for crying seven years after this man was out of her life. But the loss of her husband still hurt. Maybe after twenty years she won't cry anymore. Or it might always be hard.

She knew her ex-husband was not good for her. But she did not want to let him go. And regardless of how you look at it, that will break your heart.

Anthony

Sometimes it's a choice of what kind of grief you want to experience. Do you want the pain of holding on or the pain of letting go?

I also had to deal with that when my mom was sick. I was holding on so tight. As she got sicker, it became harder to hold on and not feel selfish, because she was suffering so much.

I remember sitting at the table with my mom one night, watching as she faded away right in front of our eyes. I cried out, "God, I need mercy, for real." There was no way I could handle watching my mother's decline.

I thought God's mercy meant that He would heal her completely and take away all the pain. That's not what happened, but I still received God's grace—in the time I was able to spend with my fa-mily before COVID hit and in the sweet moments we all had together because we were forced to slow down.

My dad was worried I wouldn't be able to handle losing Mommy, that I would completely tank emotionally. But he saw how I grieved, and I believe it helped him with his own grief. God's mercy became real to me in a way it had never been before.

Stacy

No one can give you a detailed map through grief. It's universal and yet very personal for each one of us. It's important to identify what a loss means to you—whether it's the loss of a loved one in death, loss of a relationship or job, loss of a dream, or loss of anything, for that matter. Get your feelings out by writing them down. Talk to someone about it. How did the loss impact you? Why are you feeling what you feel?

Many of us speak to God about our pain and loss, and that is good too. Putting emotions into words can be healing. Refuse to let anyone tell you how you should feel. Your feelings are yours. Own them.

Anthony

What can we say to somebody who is so deep in grief and loss that they feel numb?

Stacy

Let's go back to that gym metaphor from earlier. A person who lifts weights will eventually build up calluses on their hands. If you stick a needle in that callus, it won't hurt because the body has built up a rough patch that protects them from the pain.

Our hearts do the same thing. The pain can become so overwhelming that we build up walls. It's important to realize there are feelings behind the walls. Eventually the dam will break.

That's another situation where therapy can be helpful. We help remove the callus and slowly release the pain so a person can be healthy and whole again. Emotional support is key, especially from someone who has walked in your shoes. That's where groups such as DivorceCare and Celebrate Recovery come in. They gather people together who are going through a similar type of loss. Many of these support groups meet in your local church or synagogue. Nobody will understand your pain like someone who has been there.

Of course, you can also find support from someone who cares but hasn't walked in your shoes. The important thing is to reach out to connect with someone who can be there for you during a difficult time.

Anthony

What about the famous order to the stages of grief?

Stacy

These tips, much like grief, aren't in any sort of order. You may have heard about the stages of grief first labeled by a psychiatrist named Elisabeth Kübler-Ross, which are denial, anger, bargaining, depression, and acceptance. We all have different experiences, though, and not everyone experiences all of them. And those stages we do experience are in no guaranteed order.

Denial does often come first, but not for everyone. I was in denial about the onset of the pandemic. I thought everything would be back to normal in two weeks, so I didn't run out to get toilet paper. When I did finally venture out to the supermarket, guess what I found? Empty shelves. Then came anger.

Bargaining isn't like negotiating to get a discount at a garage sale or flea market; it's when we face a loss and beat ourselves up with all the things we should've, would've, or could've done to make it different.

When it comes to bigger losses, like the loss of a loved one, we are in denial thinking things like, *Can they really be gone?* and we bargain with phrases like *I should have seen them more.* Plus, we feel emotions like anger and depression when we feel like their passing was unfair or too soon.

Anthony

I'll add something that helps me with bargaining. I have always tried my best to live life in the moment—whatever is in front of me. If I sing, I sing like there is no tomorrow. If I see my friend or family member, I'm going to tell them how much I love and appreciate them because none of us are promised another day.

When my mom got her diagnosis, I made the most of every moment and was sure to enjoy whatever time we had left, but thank God I had been living that way all along. The grief is still a bear, but it does help to know I lived in those moments and didn't waste time or take it for granted.

Stacy

So how do you balance the emotion of grief with the reality if you are a sensitive person?

Anthony

In the movie *Inception*, Leonardo DiCaprio would sleep and go into worlds where he wasn't sure what was real and what was only a dream. He kept a top in his pocket and would spin it whenever he felt uncertain. If the top fell over, he was in the real world.

My father is like the top in the movie. When I am lost in grief or emotion, I can look to him for a reality check.

Stacy

When it comes to grief and loss, something I shared previously still applies: a negative thought and a positive thought cannot coexist at the same time. If you catch yourself spiraling down into sad thoughts, try to divert your attention to gratitude or blessings. Help someone. Read a good book. Call a friend. Keep a list of Bible verses you can remember and think upon during difficult times. That doesn't mean you shouldn't give yourself time to feel those sad feelings—you should do that too. Just have your own version of a "top" that you can look to for balance.

Anthony

Thank God I grew up hearing Bible stories and verses all the time, because that's what kept me from getting too far down. In a car your seat belt doesn't lock in and the airbags don't come out until there is danger present. That's what the Word of God did for me. I remembered verses like Psalm 9:9, which says, "The LORD is a refuge . . . in times of trouble." Jesus told us in Matthew that those who grieve are blessed because He will comfort them (5:4). When danger came, God's truths kicked in.

When I felt weak, this scripture would go through my heart and mind: "The joy of the LORD is your strength" (Nehemiah 8:10). When I felt overwhelmed with sadness, I would say the words out loud to remind myself: "Weeping may stay for the night, but rejoicing comes in the morning" (Psalm 30:5).

The impact of grief could have permanently wrecked me, but I kept holding on to God's Word and believing that He would do what He said.

I kept trusting that "no eye has seen, . . . no ear has heard" what waits for us on the other side of this pain (1 Corinthians 2:9).

Talking about it helps too. It feels like I am honoring my mom and handling grief the right way rather than prolonging the pain. There's a hope in knowing you did things right. That's what my mom would have wanted—to use a situation that was hurtful to help someone else.

If I can do it, anybody can. I believe that with all my heart.

———— STACY'S TIPS TO HELP YOU GET STARTED

- **REFLECTION:** Reflect on the people and experiences that have led you to feel grief and loss. If someone you cared about has passed, allow yourself to reflect on the meaning they had in your life. If your pain has come from other heartaches like a breakup, loss of a job, illness, or anything else, allow yourself to reflect on why you are feeling that pain and what you might need to help heal it.
- **REALIZATION:** It is important to know that grief and loss are part of life. Have compassion for yourself. Ask yourself who or what can provide you some comfort during difficult times.
- **ACTION:** Many of us do not allow ourselves proper time to grieve. Here's what you can do to begin:

  - Sit on the floor or your bed with a box of tissues and let the sadness and pain come out.
  - If you are grieving the loss of a loved one, think about the legacy they left for you and how you would like to continue to carry that legacy in your life.
  - If you have lost a job or relationship, think about what lessons you may have learned. Also think about your future jobs or relationships. What would you like them to be like? What would you like to be the same? Different?

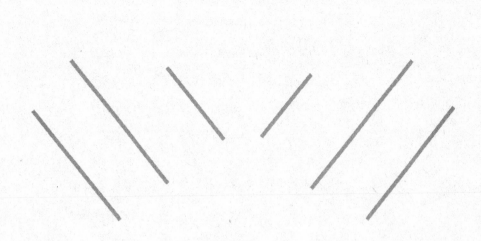

THE MORE YOU LOVE, THE MORE YOU WILL GRIEVE.

FIFTEEN

UNLEASH YOUR INNER POWER

God did not give us a spirit of timidity or cowardice or fear, but [He has given us a spirit] of power and of love and of sound judgment and personal discipline [abilities that result in a calm, well-balanced mind and self-control].

2 TIMOTHY 1:7 AMP

Anthony

"You know what to do."

If I heard my mom say that once during my young adult years, I heard her say it a hundred times.

My parents taught me everything I know about life, faith, and general decision-making, and over the years, when I would tell my mom something I was going through, that would be her response. She was basically saying, "I believe in what I've invested in you, and if you'll stop, think, and trust yourself, you'll know where to find your answer. I'm actually not going to tell you on purpose. I want to help you build strength and the knowledge of where to find these solutions that I made sure are hidden in your heart." (What's so crazy is that at times, because of all the time we spent together, I can actually *hear* my mom's voice in my head and heart, even though she is no longer physically with me.)

This is what we mean when we say your inner power. You have all you need inside you. It's just a matter of you finding it and then having the confidence to go do what you know to do.

Stacy

I struggled with not feeling my inner power when I was in middle school and I had to carpool with a kid I'll call Tommy, the son of a family friend. Sitting together in the back seat of his parents' car on our way to school, he would tease me mercilessly. I would try to defend myself, but he was sharp-tongued and quick, and I was no match for his insults. Additionally, he was my elementary school crush, and so if I am being honest, even in middle school I got tongue-tied around him. I also was sort of shy and hadn't yet developed the skill of standing up for myself, so I just took what he dished out. Five days a week I felt powerless against his attacks. I could not escape my tormentor. Many afternoons I walked through the front door of my house in tears.

I tried petitioning for my parents' help. "Oh, his father is a therapist," my mom would offer. "I don't think little Tommy would do such a thing. I bet he just has a crush on you."

It was not a misunderstanding. He didn't have a crush on me; he had a crush on my friend Emily. I couldn't change him, but the experience did begin to change me. I became quieter, started to feel like maybe something was defective inside me that caused him to do this. One of my friends eventually noticed the change.

"Stacy, why are you walking around all hunched over and withdrawn?" she asked.

Tommy had affected my inner sense of power. I couldn't find my voice. I was shrinking and getting smaller by the day. Back then I didn't have an understanding of toxic people, but now I can tell you that it was never about me; it was always about him and his need to make people small. I was an easy target because I didn't stand up for myself.

Anthony

Growing up can be brutal, and I'd guess that many of us have a story that involves being pushed around and being made to feel small, whether it was riding the bus on the way to and from school, trying to find a friend to sit with at lunch, or hoping to be chosen for a sports team. Feeling powerless and vulnerable seems to be part of the human experience.

Stacy

Yes. But as you know, these issues don't just happen in middle school. We deal with relational dynamics and difficult people every day of our lives, so it's important we address the situations and issues we face and figure out what's going on. We must learn how to live from a strength that comes from beyond the physical realm of who we are.

Anthony

"Live from a strength." I like that! It reminds me of Ephesians 3:20–21, which says, "To him who is able to do immeasurably more than all we ask or imagine, according to his power that is at work within us, to him be glory."

These verses tell me that power for living is something that comes from God. When we put our hope and trust in Him, He puts His power within us. It's like at church how we talk about not letting the temporary things determine our days—things like our position, our money, our possessions.

When we live in God's power and not our own, we see that what we have are gifts from God. It's about recognizing the source for both strength and blessing that gives us access to more than we can imagine on our own.

Stacy

We often find inner strength by connecting to God and others. I love seeing how Anthony's foundation of faith, along with his friends and family, has given him inner strength. When he started to feel like he was on shaky ground, he reached out to me, to his faith, and to his family. Then he began to reach out to friends for help and encouragement.

It's important to have sources of strength to draw upon whenever we feel weak.

Anthony

I shared earlier about a time that I came into Stacy's office overwhelmed. Actually, to be honest, I was crying my eyes out—just a wreck. I felt completely out of control and totally powerless. Though Stacy normally sits in a chair across from her clients, that day she asked if she could sit next to me. She later told me that she sensed I felt all alone, and that I was struggling so deeply I likely thought even God was not with me. She began to point out specific instances where she had noticed He indeed was evident in my life through those hardest times.

Though I couldn't see or find any power of my own, He sent an extension cord, Stacy, to me to help me connect back to Him.

Stacy

If a compassionate person sees someone in pain, they move closer—either physically or emotionally. I've seen Anthony do that as well. He wants to share whatever strength he has to help the other person back up on their feet. Strength can come through physical, emotional, or spiritual support.

Anthony

The Bible is such a lifeline to me. In fact, all the verses we've used in this book I have used to encourage myself in hard times. Especially when I feel weak and full of doubt. On those days I remind myself that 2 Timothy 1:7 says the Spirit of God does not make us timid. He has given us power, He loves us, and through that love and power we have self-discipline and a sound mind.

These verses are essential, but it helps to have other people to encourage and remind us too.

Stacy

That's why I keep encouraging others about the importance of a good support system—a friend, family member, pastor, counselor, or even a person you connected with on social media. You need someone to remind you that you are not alone in the struggle. There is strength in numbers, and that is why support is so important.

Anthony

I was thinking about struggle this morning while I was on the treadmill. Does everybody hate the treadmill as much as I do? It doesn't make any sense to me. There I was working hard, sweating, running fast . . . and going nowhere. Thirty minutes later I was in exactly the same place as I was before. That's frustrating.

Sometimes I feel like I'm on the treadmill of life, working and sweating but not really getting anywhere. Now, when I think of stressful times, I see them as the cardio machines at the gym. That's when God is conditioning me, making me stronger, building up my strength and endurance.

Even though it feels like I haven't made any progress, my heart is being conditioned. I will have more power and strength to endure because I learned to trust the process and push through.

You are holding the proof of that right now. Doing a project like *When Faith Meets Therapy* was a big dream of mine, but I was only able to make it happen by going through those difficult times—by trusting and pushing through until I was strong enough to not only help myself but help others as well.

Second Corinthians 4:16–17 talks about how we do not lose heart. Though the outside seems to be wasting away, we are inwardly being renewed day by day. That's what I was thinking about on the treadmill. The outward appearance looks sweaty and fatigued, but on the inside, power is being renewed by light and momentary troubles.

Trust me. The glory that waits for us far outweighs the trouble we are going through now.

Stacy

Anthony is the king of illustrations.

Anthony

I am my father's son.

Stacy

It's important to identify sources of power and inspiration. On vacation in Portugal, touring old buildings, I went into an old church. It wasn't even a church anymore—just an empty building. But I could sense the presence of God and a power there, something I wanted to hold and carry with me. It gave me strength because I could feel the power of spiritual support. That moment brought me to tears, the kind of tears that come from the joy of knowing a presence is with me and I am not alone.

I can still feel that power even today.

Anthony

There have been so many days when I've come into therapy with a heavy heart. At this point, I know you might be thinking that I'm making myself sound pitiful, but I want to make sure y'all see it as it really was and understand that I'm not just delivering a sermon about struggle here. I've been there too.

I was sitting there with my head down, trying to find a way to even put what I was feeling into words.

After Stacy came over and sat in the chair next to me, she said, "In all my years of therapy, I have never seen someone so covered by God." I walked out of her office with my head up and a new reality to hang my hat on. It was exactly what I needed to hear.

I hope she wasn't making that up just to make me feel better!

Stacy

No, I remember that day. This might sound crazy, but there was this glow around him. I could really see it. I told him that. It was another moment when I felt the presence of God. I knew He was there with us.

Anthony was in a dark place, wondering, *Where is the light?* God let me see His light and I was able to point it out.

Anthony

You know what? All of you reading this book—you are covered too! Acts 10 says God doesn't play favorites (v. 34). He is with us in our lowest moments. Maybe you don't have anyone to talk to or trust with your deepest pain. Maybe you feel like you are too far gone or too messed up to ever heal. Maybe you picked up this book hoping to find some small word that would make you not feel so down. Maybe you're just trying to get through this day.

God is with you, even if you can't see the light. Even if you feel a million miles away. You are covered by grace and God's love.

Stacy

Amen, amen. Beautiful.

Let me bring this full circle. Remember Tommy, my childhood tormentor? About five years ago, he reached out to me on social media and sent something like this:

> Hey Stacy, you were a significant part of my childhood,
> so I wanted to reach out. I just wanted you to know, I'm
> a therapist now. I see that you're a therapist, too, and
> thought we should connect.

I wasn't sure if I wanted to have a conversation with Tommy and bring back all those terrible feelings again. He was so awful to me. Could someone really change that much?

We met at a coffee shop. Years had passed, and I wasn't so meek and quiet anymore. I found my voice and knew how to use it, letting him know just how much his words had hurt me, the teasing and terrible things he'd said, all the days I'd cried and dreaded school, how sometimes I could still feel that hollow dread in the pit of my stomach.

All those old emotions came pouring out. I cried, and to my surprise, Tommy broke down too. It was kind of awkward but also sweet; in the end he apologized and said he had no idea that he'd caused me so much pain. He also shared with me that he was being bullied, too, and that he was making himself feel better by making me feel small. Of course he had no idea that he was doing that back then. But it made me remember the concept that hurt people hurt people.

Then I told him the other side—that even though he had been so cruel, he had taught me a lesson about taking my power back with people who tried to hurt me, and that his willingness to meet me all these years later helped me do that with him. The experience also gave me a heart for the helpless and compassion for those struggling and down. I wanted to help others who felt that way.

Anthony

Every now and then, life offers us a bit of closure. Sometimes, though, you have to seize the moment and help that closure come your way.

Stacy

I have a dog named Riley, a feisty little terrier mix that we rescued about five years ago. Every night I take him out for a walk before bed. That is my quiet time with God, when the streets are dark and still. I walk and pray out loud, looking at the stars in the night sky. That's where I do my best thinking, when the little epiphanies come that carry me through. Really, it's one of the best parts of my day. I take those moments to pray and to think about what I can do personally in my life to make things better. I both relinquish control and feel control at the same time.

For those of us who wake up in the middle of the night, that's a good time to connect and listen too. But the important thing is that you find the time that feels best for you.

Anthony

Connect and *listen* are verbs. Action. Being still doesn't necessarily mean that you have to be motionless. Sometimes power requires action.

Many Bible stories tell us how God's people connected to His power by being faithful in small, seemingly insignificant actions. Moses and the children of Israel were stuck in a dead end at the shore of the Red Sea with Pharaoh's army coming in hot, ready to bring them back into captivity.

God said to Moses, "Raise up your rod" (my paraphrase).

I would have been thinking, *Really, Lord? What good is this walking stick going to do against an army? Can't You just send another plague of locusts? Or better yet, just part this sea without asking me to do anything.*

But Moses listened and obeyed God's command, and because of that he was used in a way he could have never imagined. Through his obedience, not only did he escape bondage, but everyone who was with him also experienced deliverance. God's decision to part the Red Sea for thousands started with the obedience of one man. One man who initially felt underqualified (Exodus 14).

Stacy

If you are listening to God and listening to yourself, faith has now met therapy. So often we stop listening to one or both. We need to make a conscious effort to listen to both. To take our power where we can and give power over to Him as well.

Anthony

And that is the truth. Sometimes as believers we might think listening to yourself means you're not listening to God. Well, if you've hidden His Word in your heart, guess what? It's one and the same. Like what my mother used to say to me—"You know what to do." The moment you learn how to resort to what is hidden in your heart is the moment you learn how to trust and therefore live in and at peace with God and yourself.

Let's say you are stuck at the shore of your own Red Sea. The army is coming up behind, and you are feeling weak and scared. How do you find the power to move forward without doing something foolish out of anxiety and fear?

Stacy

I think God sends signs; we just have to be willing to listen, watch, and learn. I tell people to try different paths and see where the doors are opening, where things are working out. If the doors keep closing, you need to pay attention to that too.

I was talking to a client today who had been looking for a relationship and finally met not one but two men who wanted to go out with her. A blessing, yes, but she was conflicted about how to deal with this windfall.

"Should I tell one of them no?" she asked. "I've never dated two people at the same time before."

"Take it slow," I told her. "You just met them both. Go down the path a bit. Have dinner. Talk. Take a walk together. See what happens before you make any decisions. It's okay to not know right now. Just take it day by day."

After the first couple of dates, one of the guys started showing his true colors, criticizing her diet, making little, petty, cutting remarks. His first impression was charming, but he got annoying fast. My client was watching for red flags like that, though. He weeded himself out for her. Now she has one path, one guy, and he's turning out to be pretty amazing!

That's a very simple example, but I think career and friendships work that way as well. Take it step by step. Keep your eyes and mind open. Watch for the signs. Do the work on your end.

Anthony

Early in my singing career, it seemed like every door of opportunity kept closing in my face. Nashville meant well but kept trying to make me into something I wasn't, just to fit the market. I said yes to them picking out my clothes, my songs, my sound. I was even presented holding a guitar when I didn't even play. None of it fit me and I felt foolish, but I wanted success so badly that I was willing to compromise. Being a people pleaser didn't help either. The signs were all around me, but I refused to see them.

Through all that frustration, God was leading me toward something better. Because I kept moving forward in spite of the holdups, I was picking up skills along the way, learning from my mistakes, figuring out not only who I was but also who I did *not* want to be. The process was uncomfortable. Doors closing in your face can and will drain your confidence and power.

But as I started to be still before God, to listen and watch for the signs, the path became clearer. When that happened, my confidence came back. The more I moved forward, the more I realized that God was making it clear: I wasn't supposed to be following someone else's path; I was supposed to be clearing my own.

Real power is simply confidence in ourselves and having even more confidence in God's willingness to help and guide us along the way. Like the scene I talked about with Simba and Mufasa, it's knowing that God has got our backs and our attempts at "roaring" will inevitably be met with His.

Stacy

Five years ago, neither of us would have ever believed that we would be writing a book together about facing fears, dealing with relationship issues, and unleashing our inner power. It happened step by step. Anthony reached out to me and took a chance on the process. Our first session was productive, so he scheduled another one. The doors kept opening, so we continued on. And here we are today.

Human nature wants the process to be easy and obvious. But life doesn't always work that way. Most of the time it takes work. But that work, and the results you get from the work, help make you feel stronger and more powerful.

Anthony

When the Bible says ask, seek, knock (Matthew 7:7–12), to me, that's a big part of the plan right there. You can't just sit back. God says take action; don't wait for the doors to magically open. Sometimes you have to find the door, and then you have to knock on it. That can be exhausting, but welcome to life on earth.

A lot of people wish they could have a ministry like Dr. Tony Evans, Priscilla Shirer, Chrystal Evans Hurst, or Jonathan Evans. Just because my family have what they have now doesn't mean it came easily. My siblings and father had to ask, seek, and knock on a lot of doors before they found the way that was right for them. My family still has to be faithful to the path God has laid out and not follow one based on the pressures of what other people want them to do.

Early on, my dad was blocked and told no simply because of the color of his skin. Priscilla had to make decisions about what and who to allow into her life based on her own needs and values. Chrystal had to overcome adversity and the pressure of being a single mother at nineteen. Jonathan had to push through having trouble early on with learning and retaining information. And me, I had to work to overcome a propensity for anxiety and depression. We all have had to realize that God has placed innate access to His power in each of us. Even if it means it's just the power to take the next step.

For example, as many of you know, Priscilla is in high demand as a speaker, but I've seen her be the queen of the word *no*. Just the other day, she said to me, "Anthony, my heart won't allow me to say yes because my three boys—your three amazing nephews—only have one mom. They cannot go find another one. The biggest conference in the world can find another speaker, I promise. My voice cheering my boys on from the stands, my hands making them their fifth meal of the day, or my place at the table cannot be filled or replaced with another option. I will not leave my seat empty as a mother. That is my first calling."

Power is also knowing when to push and when to pull back. I see that in both of my big sisters. Neither of them wear themselves out going around the world doing thirty speaking engagements in thirty days. God did not call them to do everything. In a lot of cases God has first called them, as well as you, to do the *one* thing He has placed right in front of you on any given day. It could be as simple as just spending uninterrupted and focused time with Him.

Stacy

That is a great example. Those ladies know themselves. We all need to know who we are—our strengths and our limitations. Power comes first from a place of knowledge.

Anthony

First Corinthians talks about how Christ is the power and wisdom of God (1:18–2:16). From a racehorse to a race car, power is a dangerous thing if you do not have the wisdom to harness and guide it. So when you seek power, there's risk, but not just foolish risk. You've thought it out.

Stacy

We talked about fear in a previous chapter. Fear is not the lack of courage. True courage is feeling fear and doing it anyway. Don't allow what scares you to paralyze you. Small baby-steps will get you there.

Anthony

Even the greatest gymnast of all time, Simone Biles, didn't do her signature one-of-a-kind moves on day one. She has four skills named after her and thirty-two Olympic and world medals because she realized and took full advantage of how she was naturally built, looked for the best place to utilize her power, and then took the first step![8]

Stacy

Strength, energy, and a sense of power can all come from self-care. Take care of yourself—mind, body, and spirit.

And remember that one of the best ways to hold on to your power and keep the motivation to push yourself is to focus on the positive instead of the negative. Many of us spend too much time and energy thinking about what we didn't do, what is wrong with us, and where our weaknesses are. Instead, focus on your strengths, your successes, and your ability to create changes that will make your life better.

Anthony

What will make my life better? Myself. Working on me. Working with God to change. Not getting hung up on the failures of the past or what I wish I would have done.

So let me encourage you to keep your perspective fixed on the present and the future. Look forward, not back. Move on into the next moment that God will work together for your good (Romans 8:28). Pray along the way that He will show you the way, step by step, with power and wisdom and love.

STACY'S TIPS TO HELP YOU GET STARTED

- **REFLECTION:** Think about times when you have felt powerful and powerless. When you felt powerful, why was that? What was working for you? What resources and strengths did you use?
- **REALIZATION:** Knowing who you are, where you are currently, and where you want to go are all important elements of feeling empowered and in charge of your own life. Spend time on a regular basis thinking about all these things.
- **ACTION:** Achieving inner power involves a desire to take ownership

over your life and the elements in it. Make note of these three main steps:

- Evaluate: Take time to regularly evaluate your life and how you are living it so you can see what you are happy with and what needs work.
- Set Goals: Based on your evaluation, begin to set small and large goals so you can make a strategy to improve your life. For example, if you have evaluated your life and decided that you don't like your financial situation, set small goals like only allowing yourself one meal out a week, setting aside a certain amount of money each week for savings, or making sure you give more homemade gifts than purchased ones. Then, larger goals might be looking into a new job or supplemental income, or finding smart investments or a high-interest savings account to put your money into over time.
- Maintain: Monitor your action steps and goal-setting so you continue to maintain a good rhythm and system. It takes weeks or months to change a behavior, so you need to keep on yourself to make new changes stick. Part of maintenance will include praising yourself and also finding support from others who can cheerlead you along your journey.

REAL POWER IS HAVING CONFIDENCE IN YOURSELF AND EVEN MORE CONFIDENCE IN GOD'S WILLINGNESS TO HELP AND GUIDE YOU.

SIXTEEN

CHANGE EVERYTHING WITH GRATITUDE

*Consider it nothing but joy, my brothers and sisters,
whenever you fall into various trials. Be assured that
the testing of your faith [through experience] produces
endurance [leading to spiritual maturity, and inner
peace]. And let endurance have its perfect result and
do a thorough work, so that you may be perfect and
completely developed [in your faith], lacking in nothing.*

JAMES 1:2–4 AMP

Anthony

When I was a kid, my dad would take me to see our family pediatrician, Dr. Denny. Like most children's medical visits, some of mine included shots. I would be bawling my eyes out before we even went to his office, thinking about that big, long needle and how much it was going to hurt.

Dr. Denny, who I'm sure was accustomed to dealing with kids like me, would put me up on the table and open his secret drawer. This drawer was full of sweet distractions, everything from colorful Life Savers to Laffy Taffy and SweeTarts. He even had those cool Ring Pops. I would always slowly stop crying so I could see though my tears to choose my favorite, the Ring Pop! Once I slid that thing on my finger, my whole perspective would change. My mind was focused on the sweetness to come rather than the pain of the moment.

Stacy

I have a similar memory, but maybe that's not a coincidence. When I was a child, my dentist had a treasure chest in front of the chair with a bunch of toys in it. While he was drilling my cavity, he would say, "Look at the treasure chest while I'm working, Stacy. As soon as I'm done, you can go pick out a toy—any toy you like. And if you really behave, I'll let you pick out two."

Bad teeth run in my family, so I had a lot of cavities as a kid. I got to learn that lesson many times. It worked. The whine of the dentist's drill would be ringing in my ears, and what felt like smoke would be coming out of my mouth, but I would stay fixated on that chest full of tiny Barbie dolls, strawberry scratch-n-sniff stickers, Slinkys, and Weeble figurines. Does anyone remember the Weeble people? "Weebles wobble, but they don't fall down." (If you look, there's a lesson in everything.)

I wanted those toys so badly that I was more focused on the positive than the negative. That's how gratitude works. It helps us focus on the good things.

If we're going to talk about gratitude, we need to discuss gratitude within ourselves and gratitude toward others.

Anthony

Working with Stacy has taught me a lot about perspective and gratitude, about choosing to look at what I *do* have when my emotions want to focus on everything I do *not* have. I've learned that gratitude doesn't take my problem away; it just changes the way I look at the problem.

Remember the story in 2 Chronicles 20 where King Jehoshaphat pleaded with God to help him in battle? The enemy's attack would be way too much for his army to handle. In that moment, instead of instructing His people to get their armor and swords, God told them to praise Him. If my enemies were descending on me, I would be so confused by that instruction. But the story unfolds to tell us that when the people praised Him, the Lord allowed it to create so much confusion among the enemy armies that they ended up ambushing and destroying each other. God used His people's gratitude not only to help them but also to confuse and defeat their enemies!

The same can be true for us. When the battle intensifies, your gratitude should increase all the more.

Stacy

If things are not going well for you, how do you turn to gratitude? For instance, if someone's getting on your last nerve, how do you turn toward gratitude for them?

As a therapist, I believe we should all practice gratitude daily. Especially on the challenging days.

Anthony

Sometimes you're being thankful for something that's not in your hands yet—for the ability, for health, for the opportunity to even try. I'm not where I want to be in every area of my life yet. None of us is. But I am grateful for clarity and the desire to change, for a relationship with God, to know that He is on my side.

Gratitude opens our eyes and ears. It helps us to turn our attention from the negative and focus on our blessings instead.

Stacy

Anthony has experienced so much loss in the last few years. And yet he expresses gratitude about the good that came out of those trials. He's talked about things that his mom and other family members, who are now gone, have brought into his life, and the legacies he continues to carry forth because of those people.

When life is hard, one of the best things we can do is to take time to think about anything that we can be grateful for.

I feel like this pandemic has brought us back to a place of thankfulness, causing us to look around at the small things that many of us normally take for granted. People were quarantined in their homes, fearful of disease, of death, of financial ruin. As things finally began to loosen up, many of us came out with a new attitude.

I've heard people say, "Well, thank God we had Netflix. Thank God there's food in the fridge. I'm grateful that I even have a job, that I'm not on a ventilator in the ICU." Difficulties and traumas will change your perspective.

I grew up without a lot of money. My father was also raised without much, which is why he is very careful about how he handles his funds, shopping for bargains and using coupons wherever he can. For instance, if Tide is on sale he will buy three giant bottles, but only if he has a coupon to go along with the sale. He still has a stockpile of household items in his garage that we call M's Minimart, full of things he has bought at a deep discount.

We used to give Dad a hard time about that—that is, until the pandemic hit. Then we all needed to shop at the minimart because when the store shelves were bare, he had cases of toilet paper, toothpaste, and whatever else we might need.

I don't get annoyed about my dad's stockpile anymore. I was so grateful he had all that toilet paper and all those Clorox wipes. I was thankful for the very thing that has gotten on my nerves. What happened? My perspective changed.

Anthony

Everything we have talked about in this book—pursuing hope, learning how to deal with anger and pain, turning from fear, leaning into healthy relationships with forgiveness and grace—is best considered at the intersection of faith and therapy. And the starting place? It should always be gratitude.

That's why we wanted to tie up the book with this chapter on gratitude—because I believe God wants us to partner with Him in doing the work.

Stacy

Gratitude is fuel. It gives us energy to keep moving forward. And it also brings us peace.

Anthony

Depending on the distance I am going, sometimes I need to refuel on gratitude more than once a day. I might have to dig deep to find something to be grateful for. Sometimes it's simply for the breath I have to offer a prayer of appreciation to God.

Think about how you want to live your life from this moment on. What are your goals? What kind of relationships do you want to have? Small steps toward those goals take us away from pain and into a place of optimism and hope for days to come. There is nothing more hopeful, encouraging, and exciting than thinking about the future in light of God's promises. When I am having an Eeyore day, if I am hurt or weighed down and unsure that anything good will come, I make myself turn toward the promises of God and give thanks.

The Lord wants to provide His children with a hope and a future (Jeremiah 29:11). God began a good work in me, and He is not going to give up until it is complete (Philippians 1:6). If I am carrying a heavy burden, Jesus promised that I can come to Him for rest (Matthew 11:28).

We want to take hold of a life where we are strong enough to confront pain and move through it, because only then are we trusting God's promises and walking in what He has invited us to do.

Stacy

If we look at a lot of the stories in the Bible, we'll see where a person was suffering and God gave them tools and a pathway to change. He rarely said, "Okay, just sit there in your pain." Even when He allowed pain to happen, there was always a purpose worth pressing toward.

Scripture is about moving forward. Therapy is about moving forward. These types of similarities emphasize why the conversations in this book are so meaningful to Anthony and me.

Gratitude can be part of that progress. For yourself, it can be for a physical, mental, emotional, or spiritual attribute. You could be grateful for having a roof over your head when there are storms outside or grateful that a friend picked up the phone in a time of need.

I highly recommend that each of us create a gratitude list today, if for no other reason than to keep from having to pull something together in a time of despair. If you gather it now, you can look it over and say, "These are the things that I'm grateful for." Even in the worst of times, there are always things to be thankful for.

Then, as another tool for good mental health, we express gratitude toward others. Which ends up bringing good for us and for them.

Anthony has expressed gratitude for me throughout this book, which adds to my sense of fulfillment. I appreciate that.

Anthony

It's true. I don't know if Stacy realizes how much she's helped me, but I want to make sure to say it out loud. I have dedicated this book to the people in my life who convinced me that I was worth the work. Stacy is one of those people. She showed me things about myself that I could not see. When I think about that, it makes me get choked up . . .

Stacy

I so appreciate Anthony saying that out loud. And hey, sometimes gratitude brings good tears!

Listen, when you are grateful for someone, let them know. So many of us walk around in our own misery and fog that we forget about the impact we have on other people. With so much pain and sadness in the world, finding beauty is important. If you aren't feeling good about yourself, go tell someone how much you appreciate having them in your life. Brag on them. It will bring *you* joy to lift *them* up.

Anthony

I can't say it enough: gratitude changes everything. When hope seems thin or I am feeling overwhelmed, I rely on this promise from Isaiah 43: "Do not fear, for I have redeemed you; I have called you by name, you are mine. When you pass through the waters, I will be with you; and through the rivers, they shall not overwhelm you; when you walk through fire you shall not be burned, and the flame shall not consume you. For I am the LORD your God, the Holy One of Israel, your Savior" (1–3 NRSV).

We're getting toward the end of this book, so I'll tell one last story for the road. I was going to sing in New York City once and I was really struggling that day, feeling lost inside myself and all my problems, anxious about everything. I was singing at the beautiful Brooklyn Tabernacle, and moments before I went on, a guy walked up to me and rolled up his right sleeve. Inked in black on his forearm were these words: *Could It Be.*

"Wait, what?" I said. "Is that . . . ?"

"Could It Be" is the name of one of my songs. It's about how looking for fulfillment by giving my heart away to the wrong thing hurt even worse. How everything I was searching for was right in front of me the whole time. People typically get pop stars' songs tattooed on their arms—not worship leaders' songs. So this stranger's tattoo really had me confused. I asked him about it again.

"I was sitting on the side of the Hudson River about to jump and kill myself," the man explained. "I had my iPod on shuffle and this song called 'Could It Be' began to play. I heard your words, and it was a reminder of where I needed to search for wholeness and that I really did matter in this life. I climbed down off the bridge and got this tattoo so I won't forget."

What else could I do but wrap my arms around this man? I was so honored to be a part of his story and so happy that he realized his value. I felt so loved by the Lord in that moment! How else could this man have known how much *I* needed to hear *his* words right then? I had been struggling with the pain in my life that I had been honest about when writing that song, and in the middle of it all, that pain became a tool of healing for us both.

Wow. I needed that reminder on that specific day because I was ready to turn off my microphone for good. This man's gratitude made me grateful, so I offered gratitude back. That's how gratitude works. You pass it along and it just keeps growing.

Stacy

Healing isn't just working through your own problems. Helping others can be healing too. Action springs from gratitude. We resist sitting in our struggles. We learn to press in, pivot, and find the good.

Some adverse things you experience you will never, ever forget, but that doesn't mean you cannot change, heal, and improve your life. Good things can come from the worst of circumstances. Trauma can teach us resilience and compassion. The ability to stand back up and rebuild your life after you've been knocked down, to work toward being the person you want to be, that comes from what we do with a difficult experience.

Anthony

As we close this chapter, Stacy and I hope that something we've said will help you to get closer to God and to open your eyes to the fact that you are worth fighting for. We want you to move forward in spite of the past, to have the kind of faith that moves mountains, and to heal.

We pray that it will lead you closer to the life you were born to live.

—————— STACY'S TIPS TO HELP YOU GET STARTED

- **REFLECTION:** In this reflection, I want you to try something I suggested earlier in this chapter—begin to reflect on what you are grateful for. Reflect about people, places, experiences, and memories. Also reflect on how you use gratitude with yourself and others.
- **REALIZATION:** As you reflect on your own gratitude, take time to realize how gratitude has or has not played a role in your life. Who taught you about gratitude? Who have you taught about it? Have you infused enough in your daily life? How can you do better? How has your religion taught you about gratitude? Do you use those teachings on a regular basis?
- **ACTION:** Get started on that gratitude list and keep it up every day for a week.

  - In your notebook or journal, be sure to include all the areas in your life where you are grateful.
  - Commit to expressing gratitude to yourself and others on a daily basis.
  - Promise yourself that when you are down, you will allow yourself to feel those sad feelings, but you will also quickly treat yourself to an extra helping of gratitude so you can lift yourself up.

GRATITUDE GIVES US ENERGY TO KEEP MOVING FORWARD AND BRINGS US PEACE.

WHATEVER COMES YOUR WAY

You will have complete and free access to God's kingdom, keys to open any and every door: no more barriers between heaven and earth, earth and heaven.

MATTHEW 16:19 MSG

Anthony

The point of *When Faith Meets Therapy* is to share some key things I have learned along the way. I had to work hard and long to get those keys and wanted to write the kind of book I wished I could have read back when I first began. Some of this work we simply must do for ourselves—that's the only way it will sink in. But if I can share anything that might help someone move a little further down the road toward healing, that's what I want to do.

Well, that's what *we* want to do. Stacy Kaiser is the one who I believe

God sent to help me get unstuck and moving. She didn't just get all those wisdom keys from college lectures and textbooks, though.

Stacy

Don't I wish that people could learn how to deal with life's hard lessons by taking a class. I have walked through my own seasons of loss, broken relationships, struggles, and pain. Again, being a licensed therapist doesn't exempt you from challenges. We all have them. And none of us is handed a guidebook when we are born, so we need to learn the skills to deal with difficulties as we go along.

Studying the theories of good mental health is important, and there are a lot of keys to life that I have learned over my twenty-five-year career as a therapist. But many of those lessons could only be reinforced by walking through something difficult. Sometimes we don't learn about what works for us until we have been put to the test. For example, I had read a lot about the pain of grief, but I never truly understood it until my grandmother passed. She was one of my greatest cheerleaders, and losing her had a huge impact on my life and career. I learned that the pain would ease at times and then resurface with great force again. I would never have known that had I not lived it.

Anthony

It's one thing to sing about pain—to stand in front of hurting people and tell them to trust God in the storm. It's something else to go through the worst of pain—to watch loved ones suffer and pass away, to feel pain day and night, to see your family hurting badly too. And just when you think that pain is letting up, something else comes along to hurt you again.

I went through that recently, and I can tell you that it made my ministry deeper and my walk with God stronger, but it came at a cost. Thank God I was already receiving guidance and support. Thank God I had been working on bringing faith and therapy together to give me better tools for handling life. You know I love an illustration, so I'll share one more here at the end.

There was a time when I had so many jobs and responsibilities that I would carry this huge ring full of keys. It was too big to put in my pocket, but if I clipped it to my belt it would jingle really loud and people kept flagging me down in the hall to tell me things like, "Oh, hey, the AC is leaking on the second floor."

It was kind of awkward trying to explain why I carried this massive ring of keys if I was not a maintenance man, so I was relieved when keyless entry became a thing and I could stick all those old-school metal keys in a kitchen drawer. But one day I needed that key ring to unlock a door that did not have keyless entry. I fished through every drawer until I found the old key ring, fumbling with each key, trying to find the right one to unlock that door. My plane for Texas was leaving in three hours. I don't know if you've ever been to LAX, but it can be the closest thing to purgatory on this earth. That's one airport you do not want to try to navigate in a hurry.

I felt that old anxiety squeezing my chest and cutting off my breath as I cycled through the keys again, jamming each one into the lock, twisting and trying to remember which one fit. I used to know each key's use by heart and could unlock a door, *zip*, just that quick. But I had put those keys away for too long and forgot how to use them.

I tell you this because it's so important to identify and organize your keys for living. Keep those keys close so when there's a crisis, you don't have to go fumbling in the dark while pain and confusion attack you from every side. Know those keys so you can be ready for whatever comes your way.

ACKNOWLEDGMENTS

Stacy and I would love to thank Debbie Wickwire, Tracy Alderson, Kariss Farris, Chad Johnson, Jamie Blaine, Damon Reiss, and the W Publishing team for all of your valuable input and the work you contributed to help make this special project a reality.

SPIRITUAL HEALTH RESOURCES

Introduction: The Problem with Algebra
(verses on why you need guidance)

- Proverbs 11:14: For lack of guidance a nation falls, but victory is won through many advisers.
- James 4:6: But he gives us more grace. That is why Scripture says: "God opposes the proud but shows favor to the humble."
- James 2:22: You see that his faith and his actions were working together, and his faith was made complete by what he did.

Chapter 1: Jesus and a Therapist
(verses on finding insight)

- Proverbs 20:5: The purposes of a person's heart are deep waters, but one who has insight draws them out.
- Lamentations 3:40: Let us examine our ways and test them, and let us return to the LORD.
- Psalm 119:59–60: I have considered my ways and have turned my steps to your statutes. I will hasten and not delay to obey your commands.

Chapter 2: Add Hope to Your Faith

- Hebrews 11:1: Now faith is confidence in what we hope for and assurance about what we do not see.
- Psalm 34:18: The LORD is close to the brokenhearted and saves those who are crushed in spirit.
- Proverbs 29:18: Where there is no revelation, people cast off restraint; but blessed is the one who heeds wisdom's instruction.

Chapter 3: Become Your Best Self

- Romans 12:2: Do not conform to the pattern of this world, but be transformed by the renewing of your mind. Then you will be able to test and approve what God's will is—his good, pleasing and perfect will.
- 1 Peter 3:3–4: Your beauty should not come from outward adornment, such as elaborate hairstyles and the wearing of gold jewelry or fine clothes. Rather, it should be that of your inner self, the unfading beauty of a gentle and quiet spirit, which is of great worth in God's sight.
- Proverbs 3:26: For the LORD will be at your side and will keep your foot from being snared.

Chapter 4: Own It, Then Change It (verses on owning your issues and decisions)

- Romans 7:24–25: What a wretched man I am! Who will rescue me from this body that is subject to death? Thanks be to God, who delivers me through Jesus Christ our Lord! So then, I myself in my mind am a slave to God's law, but in my sinful nature a slave to the law of sin.
- Psalm 139:13–14: For you created my inmost being; you knit me together in my mother's womb. I praise you because I am fearfully and wonderfully made; your works are wonderful, I know that full well.

- Proverbs 13:20: Walk with the wise and become wise, for a companion of fools suffers harm.

Chapter 5: Face Your Fear Factor

- Isaiah 41:10: So do not fear, for I am with you; do not be dismayed, for I am your God. I will strengthen you and help you; I will uphold you with my righteous right hand.
- 2 Timothy 1:7: For the Spirit God gave us does not make us timid, but gives us power, love and self-discipline.
- 1 John 4:18: There is no fear in love. But perfect love drives out fear, because fear has to do with punishment. The one who fears is not made perfect in love.

Chapter 6: Understand the Problems and Purposes of Anger

- Proverbs 14:29: Whoever is patient has great understanding, but one who is quick-tempered displays folly.
- James 1:19: My dear brothers and sisters, take note of this: Everyone should be quick to listen, slow to speak and slow to become angry.
- Proverbs 15:1: A gentle answer turns away wrath, but a harsh word stirs up anger.

Chapter 7: Find Grace for Guilt and Shame

- Romans 5:20: The law was brought in so that the trespass might increase. But where sin increased, grace increased all the more.
- Psalm 25:3: No one who hopes in you will ever be put to shame, but shame will come on those who are treacherous without cause.
- Romans 8:1–2: Therefore, there is now no condemnation for those who are in Christ Jesus, because through Christ Jesus the law of the Spirit who gives life has set you free from the law of sin and death.

Chapter 8: Feel Your Pain to Heal It

- Proverbs 20:30 GNT: Sometimes it takes a painful experience to make us change our ways.
- Proverbs 21:5: The plans of the diligent lead to profit as surely as haste leads to poverty.
- Psalm 147:3: He heals the brokenhearted and binds up their wounds.

Chapter 9: Recognize Your Toxic People

- 1 Peter 5:8: Be alert and of sober mind. Your enemy the devil prowls around like a roaring lion looking for someone to devour.
- John 7:24: Stop judging by mere appearances, but instead judge correctly.
- 1 Corinthians 15:33: Do not be misled: "Bad company corrupts good character."

Chapter 10: Release Your Toxic People and Refocus Your Life

- Ephesians 4:31–32: Get rid of all bitterness, rage and anger, brawling and slander, along with every form of malice. Be kind and compassionate to one another, forgiving each other, just as in Christ God forgave you.
- Proverbs 26:11: As a dog returns to its vomit, so fools repeat their folly.
- Proverbs 20:3: It is to one's honor to avoid strife, but every fool is quick to quarrel.

Chapter 11: Experience Forgiveness by Letting Go

- Ephesians 4:32: Be kind and compassionate to one another, forgiving each other, just as in Christ God forgave you.

- Colossians 3:13: Bear with each other and forgive one another if any of you has a grievance against someone. Forgive as the Lord forgave you.
- Matthew 6:14: For if you forgive other people when they sin against you, your heavenly Father will also forgive you.

Chapter 12: Protect Your Peace, Then Live in It

- Proverbs 4:23: Above all else, guard your heart, for everything you do flows from it.
- Philippians 4:7: And the peace of God, which transcends all understanding, will guard your hearts and your minds in Christ Jesus.
- John 16:13: But when he, the Spirit of truth, comes, he will guide you into all the truth. He will not speak on his own; he will speak only what he hears, and he will tell you what is yet to come.

Chapter 13: The Seven Keys to Healthy Relationships

- 2 Peter 1:5–7: For this very reason, make every effort to add to your faith goodness; and to goodness, knowledge; and to knowledge, self-control; and to self-control, perseverance; and to perseverance, godliness; and to godliness, mutual affection; and to mutual affection, love.
- 1 Corinthians 13:4–5: Love is patient, love is kind. It does not envy, it does not boast, it is not proud. It does not dishonor others, it is not self-seeking, it is not easily angered, it keeps no record of wrongs.
- Proverbs 27:17: As iron sharpens iron, so one person sharpens another.

Chapter 14: Grow Through Grief and Loss

- Psalm 34:18: The Lord is close to the brokenhearted and saves those who are crushed in spirit.

- Psalm 126:6: Those who go out weeping, carrying seed to sow, will return with songs of joy, carrying sheaves with them.
- Psalm 9:9: The LORD is a refuge for the oppressed, a stronghold in times of trouble.

Chapter 15: Unleash Your Inner Power

- Ephesians 3:20–21: Now to him who is able to do immeasurably more than all we ask or imagine, according to his power that is at work within us, to him be glory in the church and in Christ Jesus throughout all generations, for ever and ever! Amen.
- 2 Corinthians 4:16–18: Therefore we do not lose heart. Though outwardly we are wasting away, yet inwardly we are being renewed day by day. For our light and momentary troubles are achieving for us an eternal glory that far outweighs them all. So we fix our eyes not on what is seen, but on what is unseen, since what is seen is temporary, but what is unseen is eternal.
- Acts 10:34–35: Then Peter began to speak: "I now realize how true it is that God does not show favoritism but accepts from every nation the one who fears him and does what is right."

Chapter 16: Change Everything with Gratitude

- James 1:2–4: Consider it pure joy, my brothers and sisters, whenever you face trials of many kinds, because you know that the testing of your faith produces perseverance. Let perseverance finish its work so that you may be mature and complete, not lacking anything.
- Jeremiah 29:11: "For I know the plans I have for you," declares the LORD, "plans to prosper you and not to harm you, plans to give you hope and a future."
- Philippians 1:6: Being confident of this, that he who began a good work in you will carry it on to completion until the day of Christ Jesus.

Conclusion: Whatever Comes Your Way
(verses for carrying on with strength)

- Matthew 16:19: I will give you the keys of the kingdom of heaven; whatever you bind on earth will be bound in heaven, and whatever you loose on earth will be loosed in heaven.
- Hebrews 10:36: You need to persevere so that when you have done the will of God, you will receive what he has promised.
- Philippians 4:13: I can do all this through him who gives me strength.

MENTAL HEALTH RESOURCES

People to Talk To

If you are looking for a therapy referral, ask friends and/or any medical professional you currently trust, or contact the psychology department of your closest college or university.

- National Suicide Prevention Lifeline: Call 1-800-273-TALK (8255)
- Crisis Text Line: Text "HOME" to 741741
- National Domestic Violence Hotline: 1-800-799-SAFE (7233) or text LOVEIS to 22522
- National Child Abuse Hotline: 1-800-4AChild (1-800-422-4453) or text 1-800-422-4453
- RAINN (Rape, Abuse, and Incest National Network) National Sexual Assault Hotline: 1-800-656-HOPE (4673)

Books to Read

David D. Burns, *The Feeling Good Handbook*, rev. ed. (New York: Plume, 1999).

Louise L. Hay, *You Can Heal Your Life* (Carlsbad, CA: Hay House, 1984).

Amir Levine and Rachel S. F. Heller, *Attached: The New Science of Adult Attachment and How It Can Help You Find—and Keep—Love* (New York: Tarcher Perigree, 2010).

Gary Chapman, *The Five Love Languages: How to Express Heartfelt Commitment to Your Mate* (Chicago: Northfield, 1992).

Lindsay C. Gibson, *Adult Children of Emotionally Immature Parents: How to Heal from Distant, Rejecting, or Self-Involved Parents* (Oakland, CA: New Harbinger, 2015).

Malcolm Gladwell, *Outliers: The Story of Success* (New York: Little, Brown, 2008).

Bruce D. Perry and Oprah Winfrey, *What Happened to You? Conversations on Trauma, Resilience, and Healing* (New York: Flatiron, 2021).

Bessel van der Kolk, *The Body Keeps Score: Brain, Mind, and Body in the Healing of Trauma* (New York: Penguin, 2014).

Margaret Paul, *Inner Bonding: Becoming a Loving Adult to Your Inner Child* (New York: HarperOne, 1992).

Elisabeth Kübler-Ross and David Kessler, *On Grief and Grieving: Finding the Meaning of Grief Through the Five Stages of Loss* (New York: Scribner, 2005).

Brené Brown, *The Gifts of Imperfection: Let Go of Who You Think You're Supposed to Be and Embrace Who You Are* (Center City, MN: Hazelden, 2010).

Russ Harris, *The Happiness Trap: How to Stop Struggling and Start Living* (Boston: Trumpeter, 2011).

NOTES

1. Stan Lee, Amazing Fantasy, no. 15 (1962), Marvel Comics; *Spider-Man*, directed by Sam Raimi (Culver City, CA: Columbia Pictures, 2002).
2. "List of 365 Fear Not Bible Verses," Hey Creative Sister, accessed March 9, 2022, https://heycreativesister.com/365-fear-not-bible-verses; "List of 365 Fear Not Bible Verses," Believers Portal, March 6, 2018, https://believersportal.com/list-365-fear-not-bible-verses/.
3. Glenn Croston, "The Thing We Fear More Than Death," *Psychology Today*, November 29, 2012, https://www.psychologytoday.com/us/blog/the-real-story-risk/201211/the-thing-we-fear-more-death.
4. Leo Newhouse, "Is Crying Good for You?" *Harvard Health* (blog), March 1, 2021, https://www.health.harvard.edu/blog/is-crying-good-for-you-2021030122020.
5. Kirsten Weir, "Forgiveness Can Improve Mental and Physical Health," *Monitor on Psychology* 48, no. 1 (January 2017): 30, https://www.apa.org/monitor/2017/01/ce-corner.
6. Kristen Anderson-Lopez and Robert Lopez, "Let It Go," performed by Idina Menzel, *Frozen* (Original Motion Picture Soundtrack), Walt Disney Records, 2013.
7. *The Lion King*, directed by Roger Allers and Rob Minkoff (Burbank, CA: Walt Disney Studios Motion Pictures, 1994).
8. "Simone Biles," USA Gymnastics, accessed February 21, 2022, https://usagym.org/pages/athletes/athleteListDetail.html?id=164887; Alice Park, "These Are All the Gymnastics Moves Named After Simone Biles," *Time*, July 26, 2021, https://time.com/6083539/gymnastics-moves-named-after-simone-biles/.

ABOUT THE AUTHORS

ANTHONY EVANS has voiced the gospel with a melodic, thought-provoking style for two decades and has emerged as one of Christian music's premier worship leaders and singer-songwriters. Along the way, he has released ten solo projects, two of which debuted at number one on *Billboard*'s Top Gospel Album charts; released his first book, *Unexpected Places*; produced numerous music videos; acted in three movies; and performed as "Beast" in Disney's Hollywood Bowl production of *Beauty and the Beast*. Most recently Anthony received his first Grammy nomination for his executive production work on the gospel album *My Tribute*. He has collaborated with his father, beloved pastor and international speaker Dr. Tony Evans; his sisters, Priscilla Shirer and Chrystal Evans Hurst; along with his brother, author and speaker Jonathan Evans, in the book *Divine Disruption,* as well as many inspirational events.

Anthony's appearance on NBC's *The Voice* led him to being discovered and enlisted to perform and produce vocals for various major artists and networks. In addition to vocal production, Anthony has been enlisted as talent producer for an assortment of popular reality and competition shows. His powerful, one-of-a-kind voice has allowed Anthony to not only vibrate the doors of the church but to make connections and venture beyond.

STACY KAISER is a Southern California–based licensed psychotherapist, relationship expert, media personality, and author of *How to Be a Grown Up*. With hundreds of television appearances on major networks including NBC, CBS, ABC, CNN, and HLN, Stacy has built a reputation for bringing a unique mix of thoughtful and provocative insight to a wide range of topics. She maintains a thriving private practice while being a much-sought-after public speaker on a wide variety of topics, ranging from work, family, and personal relationship issues to trauma, emotional growth, and community-related issues. In addition to her numerous television appearances, her expertise and perspective have been solicited by major corporations, public institutions, government agencies, philanthropic organizations, and other media outlets, including recently working on Lifetime's *Surviving R. Kelly* and A&E's *Undercover High*.

As a psychotherapist on Investigation Discovery's *Fatal Vows*, VH1's *Celebrity Fit Club*, and Facebook's *Red Table Talk*; parenting expert on the *Today* show and *Good Morning America*; and regular guest expert on *Steve Harvey* and *The Doctors* talk shows, Stacy Kaiser has gained a reputation for helping people live a more balanced and fulfilling life.

From the Publisher

GREAT BOOKS
ARE EVEN BETTER WHEN THEY'RE SHARED!

Help other readers find this one:

- Post a review at your favorite online bookseller

- Post a picture on a social media account and share why you enjoyed it

- Send a note to a friend who would also love it—or better yet, give them a copy

Thanks for reading!